Democratic Leadership in Education

Biographical details

Philip Woods is Professor of Applied Research in Education, in the Centre for Research in Education and Democracy, University of the West of England, Bristol. He has written extensively on educational policy, leadership and governance, as well as exploring issues of creative social action and governance in sociological theory. Current research includes investigation of diversity and collaboration amongst schools (including Steiner schools as an alternative form of education), distributed and democratic leadership, and the relationship and interaction of private sector entrepreneurialism and public service ethos and values in the drive to modernise leadership in education.

Democratic Leadership in Education

Philip A. Woods

Paul Chapman
Publishing

First published 2005

Paul Chapman Publishing
A SAGE Publications Company
1 Oliver's Yard
55 City Road
London EC1Y 1SP

SAGE Publications Inc
2455 Teller Road
Thousand Oaks, California 91320

SAGE Publications India Pvt Ltd
B-42, Panchsheel Enclave
Post Box 4109
New Delhi 110 017

Library of Congress Control Number: 2005924503

A catalogue record for this book is available from
the British Library

ISBN 1-4129-0290-8
ISBN 1-4129-0291-6 (pbk)

Typeset by Dorwyn Ltd, Wells, Somerset
Printed on paper from sustainable resources
Printed in Great Britain by the Athenaeum Press, Gateshead

Dedication

For Glenys

Contents

Figures and Tables

Acknowledgements

This work emerges from years of study and exploration of concerns and issues close to my heart – encouraged, stimulated and challenged by a wide variety of colleagues and friends. To name all of these would be impossible. I would like to acknowledge the support of the Centre for Research in Democracy and Education in the University of the West of England's Faculty of Education, which has enabled me to concentrate on the theme of democratic leadership – particularly Saville Kushner, Director of the Centre, and Ron Ritchie, Dean. Particular thanks are due to Peter Gronn who is a gem of a colleague; for his support and valued friendship, his humour and intellectual rigour, and for the trenchant, insightful and constructive comments he gave on drafts of the manuscript which helped to improve the ideas I have struggled to express. This book would not have come to fruition without my colleague and partner, Glenys Woods. I have benefited from her loving support and inspiration, which have been crucial to the book's development, and her insight into an elevated dimension of the human spirit which is vital in understanding the ideals of democracy and democratic leadership. Last but not least, thanks are due to Stephen and Elizabeth, my son and daughter, for their forbearance, encouragement and understanding throughout the writing of this book.

The author and publisher are grateful for permission to reproduce the following:

Figure 4.1 and the quote on p. 132, Woods, P.A. (2004) 'Democratic leadership: Drawing distinctions with distributed leadership', *International Journal of Leadership in Education*, vol 7: 1, pp. 3–26, http://www.tandf.co.uk

Figure 5.1, MacBeath, J. and Moos, L. (2004) *Democratic Learning: The Challenge to School Effectiveness*, RoutledgeFalmer, London.

Table 7.1, Ball, S.J. (1987) *The Micro-Politics of the School*, Metheun, London.

Foreword

It appears that no modern concept has been more powerfully received in the consciousness of those concerned with school reform and improvement than leadership. The importance of leadership in generating and sustaining school development and change has been highlighted and reinforced in the contemporary literature (Fullan 2001; Day and Harris 2003). Over the last three decades, the sheer volume of writing on the subject is testament to the popularity of the idea despite challenges to the very existence of leadership as a concept. For example, there are writers who argue that the popularity of leadership 'is no proof of anything' and that to take an a priori assumption of the existence of leadership is 'a poor place to begin' (Lakomski 2005: 3). Others suggest that 'it seems very difficult to identify any specific relationship, behavioral styles or an integrated coherent set of actions that correspond to or meaningfully can be constructed as leadership as important or intended' (Alvesson and Sveningsson 2003). Yet despite such criticism leadership remains firmly centre stage in contemporary discussions about organisational change and development.

At this moment the educational leadership field is experiencing a paradigm shift in terms of its current theorising. The traditional view of leadership as that associated with individual role or responsibility is gradually being replaced by alternative leadership theories that extol the virtues of multiple sources of leadership. Contemporary theorising about leadership has moved away from the traditional 'transactional versus transformational' divide into a more sophisticated amalgam of theoretical lenses. One of these powerful lenses is distributed leadership which reinforces that leadership is not the preserve of one individual. Implicit within the current discourse about distributed leadership theory is the idea that leadership is something many people are able to exercise and that leadership 'is not the realm of certain people in certain parts of the organization' (Ogawa and Bossert 1995: 225). As Lakomski (2005: 57) summarises: 'the weight of the leadership argument has been re-located from its over reliance on the leader's influence to determining relevant variants of leader influence, to findings substitutes for it and to arguing for distributed leadership practice'.

The ascendancy of distributed leadership has been prompted, in part, by new understandings about the relationship between leadership and organisational change. Here leadership is seen as a 'social influence process whereby intentional influence is exerted by one person (or group) over other people or groups to structure the activities and relationships in a group or organization' (Yukl 1994). The 'post corporate' organisation is one in which leadership is not identified with the qualities of an individual but as behaviour that facilitates collective action towards a common goal. There is also a recognition that emerging conceptions of leadership stress the need to enable entrust and empower personnel and that successful organisations depend on multiple sources of leadership.

In short, educational leadership is being redefined and re-routed towards notions of distribution where leadership permeates organisations rather than being confined to particular roles or responsibilities. Here leadership is an organisational characteristic or property that is interactive in design and relational in form and by implication it is widely shared throughout the organisation. However there are a number of questions we need to ask. Firstly, what does distributed leadership look like in practice? Secondly, how do we know it makes a difference? Thirdly, what is the extent of this difference? Simply signing up to the idea of distributed leadership without addressing such fundamental questions would seem ill advised.

Turning to the issue of democratic leadership, the same questions would apply. Is it simply the case that leadership takes on a new meaning when a new word like 'distributed' or 'democratic' is added? The leadership field is already replete with different labels for leadership and seems to generate new types, forms, definitions of leadership daily. Is there really any substance to these new leadership ideas, do they have any empirical weight and how far do they either reflect or describe actual leadership practice?

In this book Philip Woods turns his attention to issues of democracy and leadership. He has provided an eloquent, intellectually compelling and sophisticated account of a new leadership label – democratic leadership. He argues that the purpose of 'democratic leadership is to create and help sustain an environment that enables everyone who is deemed a free, creative agent to be part of ... inter-linking democratic rationalities'. Furthermore, he argues that democratic leadership has an intimate relationship with social justice insofar that democratic participation is a means of offsetting distributive injustices. His argument is carefully crafted and richly informed by a range of theoretical perspectives. The book is well grounded and challenging, making the case for an intimate connection between democracy and the creative human potential. It is benign creativity, Woods suggests, that underpins the understanding of democratic leadership in this book.

Throughout the book, democracy is anchored in a particular philosophical anthropology; it takes a particular view of what it means to be human and the potential of human creativity. Woods proposes that the aims of democratic leadership are to *share power* (by dispersing leadership) *share hope* (by extending opportunities to realise humanistic potential) and *share the fruits of society* (through fair distribution of resources and cultural respect). Most of us, I assume would readily sign up to these core aims and endorse much of what Woods proposes as democratic leadership. Understanding how democratic leadership may look and play out in practice is a challenge. Continuing research and development are required to build up the evidence base concerning the conditions that nurture, support and sustain democratic leadership practices and the educational consequences of differing styles and approaches to democratic leadership.

As the leadership field emerges from several decades of being over-shadowed by management and overlooked by policy makers and practitioners, it needs books like this to challenge, confront and inspire. There is much to be considered from reading this book and some would argue much to be contested. Philip Woods has provided a much needed alternative to the instrumental rationality and mechanistic management theories of years gone by. This is a refreshing and engaging book that will, no doubt, prompt further debate and discussion. It is a considerable asset to the educational leadership field.

Alma Harris
Series Editor

References

Alvesson, M. and Sveningsson, S. (2003) 'The great disappearing act: difficulties in doing "leadership"', *Leadership Quarterly* 14 (3): 359–81.

Lakomski, G. (2005) *Managing without leadership Towards a theory of Organisational Functioning*, London: Elsevier.

Yukl, G. (1990) 'An evaluative essay on current conceptions of effective leadership', *European Journal of Work and Organisational Psychology* 8 (1): 33–48.

Introduction

The impossibility of defining democracy is beside the mark, for though it is indefinable it is understandable, and not only by philosophers but by ordinary people.   *(Hughes 1951: 12)*

The prospects for democratic leadership look promising, at least from a cursory glance at leadership trends. Faith in the idea of the heroic, transformational leader has diminished, though certainly not disappeared. The times favour a shift towards a leadership model 'which shapes a context in which practice is made public in a collaborative culture and ... which is open to challenge, testing and refinement' (Storey 2004: 33). But this book is a work that signals caution as well as hope.

Caution is justified for at least three reasons. Firstly, the very idea of what comprises democracy is contested. Even before making any attempt to create a more democratic environment there is a danger of being confounded and diverted by the problems of defining it, or of setting out on a journey of change in the name of democracy that looks towards a destination that struggles to be worthy of that title. Secondly, the rich conception of democracy that underpins the exploration of democratic leadership in these pages necessitates an ambition and aspirations that reality will often – in fact, more often than not – fail to live up to. Thirdly, this conception of democracy challenges the dominant economistic relationships and instrumental rationality of contemporary society, and is in turn 'cabined, cribbed, confined, bound in'[1] by these social forces and existing hierarchies. Democracy demands that the world be turned upside down, but worldy powers are resilient and persistent.

Hope arises from the positive view of human nature and potential that is inherent in democratic ideals and practice. It may be difficult to define democracy, or impossible as Hughes suggests at the beginning of this chapter, but the contours and landmarks of its terrain can be drawn. Democracy is about liberty, belonging, growth towards our true potential as human beings and a unity that suffuses diversity and difference. Its practice is self-governance by equals. Its core themes are creativity and the freeing of the creative social actor to seek, with others, the truths that render life and learning meaningful.

This is an expansive conception of democracy. Other versions are possible (see Chapter 1). But they do not push us to achieve our maximum capability. Accordingly, much is demanded of democratic leadership. Its key aims are developed in this book and summarised here.

Democratic leadership aims to create an environment in which people are encouraged and supported in aspiring to truths about the world, including the highest values (ethical rationality). Leadership, therefore, as part of this, entails searching for the common human good.

Democratic leadership aims to create an environment in which people practise this ethical rationality and look for ways of superseding difference through dialogue (discursive rationality). Democratic leadership both exercises and facilitates deliberation.

Democratic leadership aims to create an environment in which people are active contributors to the creation of the institutions, culture and relationships they inhabit (decisional rationality). Democratic leadership occurs throughout the organisation and works to recognise and enhance this by encouraging dispersal of leadership. Crucially, dispersal of initiative amongst a multiplicity of democratic leaders – if it is to justify the description 'democratic' – involves the exercise of some decisional rights, such as

● exercising democratically legitimated authority; that is, making or influencing decisions as an *accountable* post-holder (acting as a positional leader);

● activating accountability processes; for example, taking the initiative as an organisational or community member to elect or hold others to account (initiating a vote and so on);

● taking the initiative in participatory, decision-making forums; for example, by initiating a debate or motion.

Democratic leadership aims to create an environment in which people are empowered and enabled by the institutional, cultural and social structures of the organisation (therapeutic rationality). Democratic leadership contributes to leaders' and others' growth towards human potential.

Democratic leadership promotes respect for diversity and acts to reduce cultural and material inequalities (social justice). These components of social justice are, accordingly, symbiotically linked with democracy.

The terrain of democratic leadership

Discussion about leadership often makes it sound as if it is purely a matter of individual will and action. However, it is important to grasp the emergent character of leadership, which we will come across in relation to distributed leadership (see Chapter 2). The broad principles of this emergent character apply to democratic leadership. Leadership is not simply a set of free-standing actions, but is also a collective property. That is, leadership comprises the impetus and direction that emerges from the group, which is more than the sum of the parts (the individuals) who make up a group or organisation. The leadership of a group or organisation comprises the direction, impetus and energy which arise from the circulation of initiative. An initiative is passed on, as it were, to colleagues who react, respond and add to the circulation, generating their own initiatives. Throughout this process there are a multiplicity of leaders engaging in actions which comprise this continual circulation.

It follows from this that the capacity for leadership lies not only within individuals, but is constituted by the institutional arrangements, culture and relationships of an organisation. Clearly, these collective, emergent properties are not disconnected from the actions of people who activate and, over time, evolve them. Hence, it is appropriate to understand leadership in terms of a trialectic framework of social dynamics (P.A. Woods 2003) involving structure, people and engagement. It is a framework that will assist in considering what is involved in creating and sustaining democratic leadership by a multiplicity of actors (see Chapters 8, 9 and 10). Figure A shows the process and inter-connections over time.

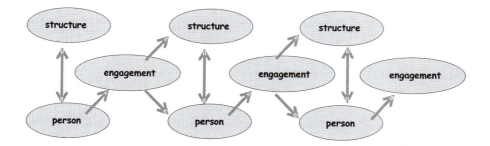

Figure A: Trialectic Framework of Social Dynamics

The *structural* properties of social life give an organisation, such as a school, some enduring characteristics which make it 'our school'. These organisational 'footprints' (enduring features of the structural environment) are the institutional, cultural and social patterns which are the product, over time, of the fleeting passage of individual social actions. Similar or reinforcing actions have a combined impact which creates institutional roles, symbols and ways of working that then have some sense of permanence. The structural properties guide and orientate people in what otherwise would be perpetually free-floating interactions of perpetually creative, but overtaxed, individuals eternally making everything anew. These structural properties have three dimensions:

- the institutional – organisational arrangements and roles, distribution of power and resources;

- the cultural – dominant or shared systems of knowledge, ideas and values;

- the social – qualities and patterns of social relationships.

The *person* is made up of the capabilities and properties of the individual, who draws from and is enabled on some occasions and, on others, constrained by the structural order in which he or she finds him/herself.

Engagement is social action which emanates from people's utilisation of and 'inner working' with the structural properties. The person draws from the structural context in which they find themselves – that is, the institutional roles and resources, the cultural ideas and the patterns of relationships. In addition, the person brings to bear his or her own interpretations on the organisational footprints others have left – interpretations which are the result of inner conversation (Archer 2003) and conversation with others. Hence there is an interactive connection shown between structure and person in Figure A. Through their engagement, people shape those same organisational structures which enable and constrain them. In a democratic organisation, these structural properties are created through the conscious participation and initiatives of a multiplicity of democratic leaders – sometimes acting as individuals, but often with others, in a process of dialogue and interaction through interpersonal connections and linkages, which may become a collective movement by a group. Democratic leadership is, assuredly, not the preserve of the one or few individuals at the apex of an organisational hierarchy.

There are two strands of dispersed leadership. There is *democracy-creating*, which involves building the conditions for and encouraging democratic processes and participation. Those in leadership positions possessing institutional authority are probably likely to be more crucial to this, though not exclusively so. Then there is *democracy-doing*, which consists of dispersed acts of democratic leadership and initiative by members of the democratic community or organisation. This includes everyone involved in debate, proposing change, collective decision making, voting and so on.

Dispersed leadership to which 'everyone' may contribute begs a difficult question about the boundary of the democratic terrain. If the aim is to build a community in which democratic leadership is the norm, what constitutes that community? Before addressing this question in relation to schools, it is worth reminding ourselves that there is a wider democratic context. Schools are situated in many countries today in national and/or regional democratic frameworks. What, from the viewpoint of the school, may look like an imposition and a restriction – such as a prescribed national curriculum – from another perspective may be seen as a nation's or region's legitimate democratic decision. It is legitimated by the process of democratic deliberation and representation. It may be challenged as undemocratic in its content if it is seen as hindering the development of creative, autonomous individuals who are the very subjects and catalysts of democracy. Or, on the other hand, such a legislative requirement on schools concerning the curriculum may be viewed by some as having benign effects on democratic citizenship and related issues of social justice. Such differences are the very stuff of democratic debate. But the point here is to emphasise that there are multiple arenas of democracy, based on different political communities. Parliaments and councils, and the national and regional communities they represent, constitute democratic contextual arenas for schools.

In relation to the question of what constitutes the school community, there are two key areas distinguishable in the literature (Furman 2002): the school-as-community where the main focus is on what goes on within the school's organisational boundary, and school-community connections where the concern is with the relationship between the school and its surrounding community. Within the school-as-community there are bounded groups also: teaching staff, non-teaching staff, students. And within these constituencies there are further distinctions – between students, for example, according to gender, social class, ethnic and cultural groupings, and so on. Democratic leadership is shaped by the product of the relationships between these constituencies and social distinctions, and the strength or openness of the boundaries between them. The pull of the pure democratic ideal is away from social distinctions towards people relating to each other as human beings. At the same time, democratic practice deals with the real conditions, distinctions and power relations that characterise everyday life.

That which Bottery urges upon the education profession as one of the constituencies in a larger democratic order, is true of each constituency, social and cultural group, and person. They have their

> understandings and expertise to share, and they should not be shy in declaring these; but they need to recognise other understandings, others' expertise, in a societal-wide debate on what is needed to improve what exists. (2004: 14)

Educational impulse to democratic schooling

The education profession has multiple accountabilities (P.A. Woods 2005). It has to take account of:

* policy hierarchies in which it is embedded – which, for instance, may involve government-mandated requirements with regard to the curriculum, pedagogy, assessment and other matters;

● market pressures – where educational institutions compete against each other for survival;

● networks – where educational institutions collaborate amongst themselves and with other agencies;

● inner (or interior) authority[2] – as a professional educator drawing on accumulated expertise and exercising informed judgement;

● communal ties – to the profession as a community, or to the traditions and values of a community (such as a religious foundation) sponsoring an educational institution;

● democratic values and democratically expressed views and preferences, where educators see themselves as democratic professionals, responsive to clients as part of their professionalism (Whitty 2002) and to an educational impulse to infuse the democratic spirit in schooling.

The exploration of democratic leadership reveals how extensive and profound are the educational implications of the last of these accountabilities (that is, an educational impulse to infuse the democratic spirit in schooling) for the aims of education and for learning and pedagogy. Democratic leadership is not only about a *responsive impulse*, which concerns leaders respecting the educational values and wishes of those they serve. Being responsive in this way, where society lays an explicit expectation on educational leaders to foster values and learning consistent with living as a citizen in a democracy, may involve provision of democratic education. But the impetus to democratic education comes equally from professional and philosophical understandings of what good education essentially comprises. In other words, there is an *educational impulse* to creating a democratic form of schooling, which derives from the accountability of the educational leaders and teachers to a sense of inner authority and to their professional community as educators, drawing on accumulated expertise and exercising informed judgement.

> [W]ith the distinguished exception of Plato, almost all notable past educational philosophers have argued for a conception of education as initiation into the kind of qualities of open-mindedness usually associated with democratic association. According to this broad consensus, ideas of education and open society are connected to the extent that there must be something suspect about any educational climate which actually runs counter to the democratic spirit. (Carr 2000: 234)

Democratic leadership implies a commitment to certain key values and ideas that are the foundation of democracy. The educational impulse to promote and nurture these is not reducible to instrumental arguments.

Education which is infused with the democratic spirit is not dependent on a rationale that views participation as being in 'the gift of management' (Bottery 1992: 167). Rather, it is integral to the educational enterprise.

An overview of chapters

Chapter 1 draws attention to the different possibilities entailed in diverse understandings of democracy and democratic leadership. Four models of democracy, based on Stokes (2002), are set out: liberal minimalism, civic republicanism, deliberative democracy, and developmental democracy. It is argued that only a profound conception of democracy and democratic leadership is tenable. The particular framework of understanding that is built up in the discussion is a developmental conception of democratic practice which is outlined in Chapter 2. This developmental conception encapsulates principles of democracy – freedom, equality, organic belonging, and substantive liberty – and the complementary, interacting dimensions of the practice of democratic leadership, comprising the ethical, decisional, discursive, and therapeutic.

Chapter 3 briefly examines the conceptual terrain concerning educational leadership, which the notion of democratic leadership needs to negotiate. In particular, attention is drawn to two key critiques that have been directed towards the influential concept of transformational leadership, in the form that has become popularised in the educational leadership field. The first is the concern that transformational leadership places too much reliance on the top leader as a 'heroic' figure, encourages manipulation of 'followers' and reinforces dependence on a dominant echelon of leaders. This has led to a much greater emphasis on the concept of distributed leadership (Bennett et al. 2003a; Gronn 2002; Woods et al. 2004). The second critique is that transformational leadership, in the way it has been translated into business and education, has developed an ethical deficit. It has lost an explicit ethical dimension of leadership. Amongst the responses to this is the formulation by Glenys Woods (2003) of a model of ethically transforming leadership. Neither distributed nor ethically transforming leadership are sufficient responses in themselves, however. To the more individually orientated model of ethically transforming leadership, democratic leadership brings a social perspective derived from intellectual roots which deal with questions of the social evolution of modernity.

With regard to distributed leadership, its narrowness and abstractness are contrasted in Chapter 4 to the breadth and richness of the concept of democratic leadership. Through the discussion and elaboration of this contrast the question is addressed as to why attention should be given to democratic leadership. The case for the importance of democratic leadership has the following components:

- intrinsic arguments, which see democratic practice as integral to a good society and intimately bound up with education, and are concerned with educational aims of creativity, inclusion and reintegration of human capacities;

- instrumental arguments, which are about its impact on student performance, engagement and self-esteem, and the organisation's capacity and ability to cope more effectively with complexity and work intensification;

- the rationale for internal alignment: namely that the style of leadership in a school should not contradict and counter the style of its teaching and learning.

The first component – intrinsic arguments – is the most essential reason to advance democratic leadership. It challenges the pressures that encourage distance between those in formal leadership positions and the human energy and capacity to be creative learners and to become goodly human. It challenges school leaders not only to recognise (which many do already) that definitions of organisational success are often the outcome of particular configurations of social and economic interests, but also to translate this recognition and questioning stance into practical implications for education. It calls on educational leadership to use and develop an empowering discourse that shapes education to genuine human need and greater ethical aims, rather than accept frames of thinking that mould people to fit the mundane passions demanded by contemporary institutions. In short, the case for democratic leadership is that it focuses school leaders on learning which is of enduring worth, by engaging them in educational issues intrinsically important to our humanity.

Schooling which is infused with a democratic spirit has, of necessity, implications for learning and relationships in the educational process. Chapter 5 considers the epistemological implications of the philosophical underpinnings of democracy: people are creators of knowledge rather than passive recipients of revealed or already-discovered knowledge. Having set out a typology of perspectives on knowledge, the chapter concludes that underpinning the educational role of democratic leadership is an open approach to knowledge. This means that understanding and knowledge develop through:

- a continual dialectical movement between a rationalist epistemology (which views certain truths as known and taken as fixed parameters of knowledge) and a critical epistemology (which considers that nothing can be taken as true and that all conceptions – all facts, theories and values – are perpetually open to critique);

- dialogue and the sharing of views, expertise and information amongst networks of learners;

- creative application of tentative knowledges in practical action.

Chapter 6 considers the link between democratic leadership and learning, from the perspectives of senior leadership, teacher leadership and democratic pedagogy. It is emphasised at the conclusion of this discussion that creating a school environment that encourages and values student feedback, and is sensitive and responsive to it, is likely to enhance learning. However, it is easy to make inflated claims about the benefits of democratic leadership and styles of schooling in terms of measurable academic results. It is important to be mindful, firstly, that examination of the research evidence reinforces the care and caution required in asserting the benefits of democratic leadership and pedagogy on academic progress. At the level of teaching, there are complex interacting principles and practices to take into account, and there is no simple connection with learning. Secondly, if students, and staff, are to be cared for as people, what school education *feels* like for students, for staff, and for families and communities is important. Dispersed, democratic leadership creates a particular texture of relationships which is supportive of all of these as creative agents with inherent potential. The human development that is integral to this texture of relationships – a sense of mutual identity and support, feelings of empowerment, social and interpersonal capabilities – is itself learning, even if not as amenable to measurement as other areas of learning. Thirdly, it is also emphasised that democratic pedagogy and practice envelop both students and staff in a school, if it is to be a community seriously committed to a breadth of meaningful learning.

Chapter 7 turns to the obstacles and challenges in the development and practice of democratic leadership. These are found in the structural context within and beyond schools, in people's attitudes and capacities, and in the practice (engagement) of democratic leadership. The succeeding chapters then address what is involved in making the journey towards the ideals of democracy and democratic leadership in schools. The discussion focuses on what this means for the component dimensions of the trialectic framework: structural properties (Chapter 8), which are the cumulative consequence of people's agency; people (Chapter 9), which concerns the capabilities and properties of individuals and the quality of relationships; and practical engagement (Chapter 10), which focuses on leaders' individual and collective agency that is enabled by and interprets and modifies the structural properties of the organisation.

Chapter 11 draws this essay into the nature of democratic leadership in education to a close. The aims of democratic leadership are summarised, though it is emphasised that no single model of democratic leadership and schooling can be advocated. The issues and characteristics identified require interpretation in local circumstances. Still, general challenges arise wherever democratic leadership is seriously pursued. In particular, there is a fundamental paradox in democratic arrangements between encouraging openness and freedom on the one hand and giving structural fixity to certain arrangements and ideas on the other. A number of dualities associated with this bivalent character of democracy require a perpetual search for balance. Nevertheless, the overriding ambition of developmental democracy is the same in all contexts, namely to enable people:

- to share power, by dispersing leadership and diminishing hierarchy;

- to share hope, by striving towards and maximising opportunities for everyone to realise the fullest humanistic potential;

- to share the benefits of living as social beings (the fruits of society), by tackling social injustices and seeking fair distribution.

Notes

1   Shakespeare's *Macbeth*, 3:4:23.
2   I have discussed 'interior authority' as an aspect of governance in Woods, P.A. (2003: 145–6).

1 Meanings of democratic leadership

The essence of democracy is how people govern themselves, as opposed to how they are governed by others (Williams 1963: 316). It is a hotly debated issue that has generated a large variety of meanings concerning the nature of democratic societies, organisations and groups (Held 1996; Saward 2003). Different conceptions of democracy imply differing conceptions of the individual and of human purposes, of norms and values and, not least, of the aims and significance of education. Some conceptions of democracy are narrow, such as liberal minimalism, one of the models of democracy discussed below. Others are broad. Carr and Hartnett, for example, describe the classical conception as a 'critical concept incorporating a set of political ideals and a coherent vision of the good society' (1996: 53) and encompassing a substantive conception of the person. This chapter, having briefly considered the origins of modern democracy in the democratisation of access to religious knowledge, discusses models of democracy which are progressively richer and more challenging, culminating in the developmental model.

A modest narrative

The origins of modern democracy lie in the recognition that neither the *capacity* nor the *right* to interpret the most important truths are necessarily confined to an elite. Indeed, seeking the true and good path came to be conceived as an obligation of everyone. The roots of the Western conception of democracy lie in the idea that the generality of people are able to detect and discriminate between fundamental values which give meaning to life and place into perspective transient, mundane passions. The religious revolution of the Reformation advanced the proposition that everyone has the capability of accessing truths about God. The notion of dispersed, individualised authority is encapsulated in Martin Luther's idea of 'a priesthood of all believers' (Hill 1975: 95). Overcoming the fear that one's salvation is in the hands of an ecclesiastical elite, to whom deference is required in order to avoid eternal punishment, paved the way for democratic ideals. As one historian put it, 'Theories of democracy rose as hell declined'.[1] And as Richard Coppin, an itinerant preacher in the seventeenth century claimed – anticipating British Idealism and the developmental model of democracy which we examine below – God is within each person, and God is both teacher and learner (op. cit.: 221). For many believers – too many – their truth became *the* final truth – the truth that everyone else ought to embrace, even be compelled to accept.

The deeper breakthrough, however, was the surrendering of theological finality and the democratisation of religious knowledge. This democratised access to truth was not intended to be an individualistic licence declaring all opinions as equally true. Hill observes: 'Emphasis on private interpretation was not ... mere absolute individualism. The congregation was the place in which interpretations were tested and approved ... a check on individualist absurdities.' (1975: 95; see also Hill 1997: 101–2)

This is *a* 'story' of a turn in social development towards democratic governance, which we should see as a *modest narrative* rather than a grand narrative.[2] There are other narratives – non-Anglo-Saxon, non-Western – about participation, shared leadership and democracy, which are to be valued and explored and which will be relevant in some or many educational contexts. For example, amongst the Bagandan people of Uganda, democracy is translated as *obwenkanya na mazima*, which means 'treating people equally and truth' and places the emphasis on being dealt with fairly and equally (Suzuki 2002). Wolof speakers in Senegal have added to the Western-derived association of democracy with elections and voting, an emphasis on consensus, solidarity and even-handedness (Saward 2003: 112–13). Islamic scholars debate the relationship between Islam and democracy, one viewpoint being that the association of the two is inevitable as Islam has an inherent theoretical affinity with the rule of law, equality and community involvement in decision making (op. cit.: 111–12). Much can be learnt from what is common and different amongst diverse understandings of democracy.

It is sufficient here, however, to note the importance of roots in the religious and political revolution of the seventeenth century. This is not because democracy has progressed steadily and smoothly from that point. Rather, what is crucial is that this modest narrative reveals the emergence of an awareness of something crucial to the idea of democracy. The modest narrative marks the breakthrough, or at least the beginnings of a breakthrough, of the *person as creative agent*. As Touraine puts it

Democracy serves neither society nor individuals. Democracy serves human beings insofar as they are subjects, or in other words, their own creators and the creators of their individual and collective lives. (1997: 19)

Moreover, democracy is anchored in a particular philosophical anthropology – a particular idea of what it means to be human and of the potentialities in human beings that make them human. For Marx, the creativity of humankind was the essential spark which made humanity what it is and, more significantly, what it could become. The problem in societies prior to the revolution envisaged by Marx is that the products of that creativity are out of human control. Humankind, most especially under capitalism, is alienated from its own character.

> Man's self-esteem, his freedom, has first to be reanimated in the human breast. Only this feeling, which vanished from the world with the Greeks, and with the Christians disappeared into the blue haze of the heavens, can create once more out of society a human community, a democratic state, in which men's highest purposes can be attained. (Marx, quoted in Lowith 1993: 108)

The essential point to hold on to does not require acceptance of the theoretical details of Marx's work, or indeed any particular religious perspective borne of the revolution in religion. Rather, the point is the intimate connection between democracy and creative human potential – and, more particularly, the potential for benign creativity. The latter is the very foundation of the broad and rich conception of democracy, which underpins the understanding of democratic leadership in this book.

The same might be said of democratic governance as Herbert Spencer said of republican governance: 'The Republican form of Government is the highest form of government; but because of this it requires the highest type of human nature – a type nowhere at present existing.'[3] Indeed, enrichment of people's lives is integral to some of the most enduring strands of democratic thinking, back to Aristotle. This principle of democracy is

> that society exists not merely to protect individuals but to offer them an enriched form of existence; so that a democratic society is one which seeks to provide positive rather than merely negative advantages to all its citizens and is to be judged by the degree to which it seeks, and is able, to do this. (Kelly 1995: 24)

Liberty for liberty's sake is not the ultimate value. Some notion of positive liberty is implied (P.A. Woods 2003). Integral to broad and rich conceptions of democracy is some sense of *unity* around universal ideals, and respect for reason and the potentialities of all people to live the good life with others. It entails the development of human beings towards some common ideal. With this there is a danger *within* democracy – a dark side we might say. An idea of positive liberty entails an idea of what is good for people, which some may then feel justified in imposing on others. Thus, what originally begins as a celebration of human identity and creativity may lead to a domination of the individual by a detailed, prescriptive and imposed conception of what the true and good path is.

Bearing this in mind, it has to be emphasised that seeking a deep conception of democracy is a delicate and demanding project. Democracy requires 'a sophisticated moral system which seeks to accommodate, even celebrate, moral and cultural diversity' (Kelly 1995: 23). A balance needs to be sought between:

- unity (around a sense of common ideals);

- liberty;

- diversity (the ideals and identities that are integral to particular groups, cultures and societies).

The defining feature of democracy is

> not simply a set of institutional guarantees of majority rule but above all a respect for individual or collective projects that can reconcile the assertion of personal liberty with the right to identify with a particular social, national, or religious collectivity. (Touraine 1997: 13–14)

Models of democracy

Table 1.1 summarises four models of democracy and their distinctive principles. These are based on Stokes (2002), who, from the array of theories of democracy, describes models which highlight the key characteristics, concerns and normative principles of the main types of democratic theory. Stokes's own outline of the models provides a starting point. In discussion of each model, I elaborate from this starting point and suggest some of the model's distinctive implications for thinking about leadership (see the right hand column of Table 1.1). The models are not entirely separate. Many of the concerns and normative principles carry forward from the narrower, more philosophically bare notions of democracy (starting with liberal minimalism) to be part of or combined with the broader notions (deliberative and developmental democracy). Hence, certain principles thread their way through all the models.

Liberal minimalism is a protective model of democracy. Its main purpose and justification is protection of the individual citizen from arbitrary rule and oppression from other citizens. Key importance is attached to procedures that curtail abuse of leaders' power, based on an individualistic conception of human beings as 'private individuals who form social

Table 1.1: Models of democracy

	Distinctive principles (based on Stokes, 2002)	Implications for leadership *Leadership...*
Liberal minimalism	Protection of individual from arbitrary rule Procedural focus: process for choosing governments Equal formal political rights Calculation/promotion of own self-interest	... is restricted to small minority ... articulates and represents interests
Civic republicanism	Civic virtue, prioritising public good over own interests Obligation to active political participation Commitment to political community	... encourages political participation and dialogue ... entails search for public good
Deliberative democracy	Enhancement of quality and use of deliberative reasoning Recognition of contemporary pluralism, inequality and complexity Regulative ideal for managing difference and conflict	... facilitates deliberation ... is dispersed amongst participants in deliberative activity ... respects diversity and acts against inequalities
Developmental democracy	Extensive political participation Enhancement of individuals' human capacities through political participation and collective state action Social justice Democratisation of civil society	... is encouraged in dispersed sites ... entails search for common human good ... contributes to own and others' growth towards human potential

relationships in order to satisfy their own personal needs' (Carr and Hartnett 1996: 43). Formal equality of political rights is emphasised and the importance of procedures for choosing governments. This brings into the frame two fundamental principles that thread through all the models. The first is political equality. Democracy is about 'the rule of equals by equals' (Kelly 1995: 6), as citizens before the law. The second is liberty, which has a dual aspect (Berlin 1969):

- negative freedom (freedom of constraint imposed by other people);

- positive freedom (the wish to be one's own master independent of external forces).

The model of liberal minimalism seeks to enable people to follow their interests in an ordered political and social framework, facilitating what C.B. Macpherson (1962) calls 'possessive individualism', which sees people as private owners of their own selves and of their own economic resources, protected by property rights (see also Olssen et al. 2004). Following Schumpeter, democratic politics is seen as 'a competitive struggle analogous to the competition of the economic marketplace' (Saward 2003: 44). It reduces democracy to a 'political supermarket' (Touraine 1997: 9). Leadership in liberal minimalism is confined to political elites competing for votes, and the main concern of leaders is to articulate and represent interests within society.

If we were to ask what is the key, distinguishing word associated with liberal minimalism, and what its prime interests-focus is, the respective answers would be 'protection' and 'self-interest'. These are shown in Table 1.2, together with the key words and the primary interests-focus of each of the other models, which will emerge from the discussion below.

Table 1.2: Key words and interests-focus of models of democracy

	key word	interests-focus
Liberal minimalism	protection	self-interest
Civic republicanism	belonging	interest of the polis
Deliberative democracy	unity in diversity	transforming interests
Developmental democracy	human potential	essential human interests

Because of the minimal democratic activity ascribed to citizens and assumptions of self-interest, an assumption shared with economic theories of markets, liberal minimalism can evolve into a notion of *consumer democracy*. If political participation is minimal, a logical step is to attach greater significance to where people are more active in modern society – namely, as self-interested actors in the market. Consumer democracy reinterprets the main focus of democracy, by shifting it from participation in politics to participation in the market. In this interpretation, people achieve influence primarily as consumers who convey their needs and preferences through their buying decisions. Such a view has influenced educational policy in countries such as the UK, New Zealand and the USA. Grace sums up well the central assertion of proponents of this view: 'Market democracy by the empowerment of parents and students through resource-related choices in education has the potential ... to produce greater responsiveness and academic effectiveness' (1995: 206). But this kind of assertion redefines democracy: 'Freedom in a democracy is no longer defined as participating in building the common good, but as living in an unfettered commercial market ... ' (Apple 2000: 111).

Civic republicanism is about belonging. It emphasises interests and concerns beyond the individual or family. Its defining features are 'the importance given to the public interest or the common good ... and [the] key role given to citizen participation' (Stokes 2002: 31). Identification with the political community (paradigmatically the nation state) is also central. Political participation by citizens is valued for its own sake. Indeed, engagement in political debates and other activities is considered a civic duty. Leadership in civic republicanism involves encouraging political participation and dialogue, and seeking to identify that which serves the public interest of the political community.

The deliberative and developmental models assimilate key features of the first two theories, such as the importance of rights and procedures that protect individual citizens (liberal minimalism) and the active role of citizen participation (civic republicanism). But they enrich democratic theory by augmenting these, as will be seen in the discussion of each of these models.

The *deliberative model* is about the collective search for unity amongst diversity. It arises from the most recent contributions to democratic theory, having been 'the dominant new strand in democratic theory over the past ten to fifteen years' (Saward 2003: 121). Its concern is that existing arrangements 'do not address sufficiently the various problems, including those of pluralism, inequality and complexity, that are a condition of contemporary society' (Stokes 2002: 39–40). Its aim is to expand 'the use of deliberative reasoning among citizens and their representatives' (p: 40) and enhance the quality of deliberation. Deliberative democracy entails individuals, in co-operation with others, seeking out the greater good for themselves and the community. This means reaching beyond one's own narrow perspective and interests, and being strengthened by this shared endeavour.

By now we have moved a long way from the competitive and minimal participation of liberal minimalism. Differences of view and conflicts of interest are recognised, but ways also have to be found to overcome them. Deliberation implies recognition of the interconnection of identity and difference. The one (identity with a national society, for example) implies the other (differences as and between local and cultural communities); identity with a group implies and encompasses differences as individuals. The point about deliberative discussion is that the realisation of unity from this difference has to be worked for. Deliberative discussion should

> deepen participant knowledge of issues and awareness of the interests of others, and help to instil the confidence to play an active part in public affairs. Deliberative democracy looks to *transform* people's (possibly ill-informed) preferences through open and inclusive discussion, not merely to design electoral procedures to *reflect* them. (Saward 2003: 121; original emphasis)

Leadership in the deliberative model involves finding ways to facilitate and sustain deliberation, which includes addressing obstacles to free and equal participation in the discourse of deliberation. In order to enable active participation by all, diversity of cultures, views and values has to be respected by those in both formal and informal leadership positions. Leadership is not confined to a small minority, unlike liberal minimalism. Opportunities for taking initiative, and responsibility for seeking out the greater good and respecting diversity, are dispersed among participants in the flow of discourse between people that comprises deliberative activity.

The *developmental model* attaches key importance to the realisation of human potential. It emphasises the positive impact that democratic participation has on personal development, and how that development is influenced or conditioned by social opportunities, constraints and relations. The intellectual roots of this model comprise the tradition which includes the Oxford political philosopher, T.H. Green, and British Idealism. Hence it views human beings as possessing inherent potentialities – for intellectual reasoning, aesthetic sensibilities, and so on – which represent the ethically good towards which it is in people's nature to aspire, provided they have a will to do so. It puts some flesh on the observation that democratic society requires a 'positive view of humankind as capable of self-directed moral behaviour' (Kelly 1995: 18).

Inherent in the developmental model is the interconnection between social action, people and the structures which order social living. It entails a view of human society which can be described as social organicism: that is, the view 'that the parts of an organism [are] mutually dependent, and thus that the value and definition of each part [is] derived from the whole; and also that the whole [is] in some way different from the sum of these parts' (Den Otter 1996: 156). This view is not meant to imply subservience of the person to the larger group. People have *both* their individual identities and interests and their unifying identity as part of the larger polity and, ultimately, humanity. The developmental model embraces the view that a cosmopolitanism which unites all is compatible with communitarianism that forges local identities.[4]

For British Idealism there is bound up with social organicism an essential *moral component*: the interconnection of self and community is essential for the genesis of the moral self. Individual and community are to be in harmonious development since the good of each person and the good of all are inherently bound up with each other. Whilst British Idealism emerges from a Christian cultural tradition, the ethical tenet at its centre is by no means unique to it. Ghandi, for example, described the same principle simply as 'the good of the individual is contained in the good of all' (1949: 250).

The developmental model implies some view of human potentiality which embraces what it means to be a good person in a good society. Realising this human potentiality is about *substantive liberty*. Substantive liberty is concerned with gaining knowledge and self-awareness which enables action in pursuit of that which is of most significant ethical value and which helps in weakening impediments to this realisation (P.A. Woods 2003). The view taken of human potentiality and of what it is to be goodly human provides a reasoned and felt understanding of what unites people as human beings. If deliberative democracy emphasises the dialogic method of reaching unity across diverse interests and identities, developmental democracy expresses the importance of a philosophical and social basis for an underlying unity which involves some substantive idea of ideals and potentialities applicable to all.

In other words, developmental democracy encompasses a sense of what it is to be human and brings an additional, unifying substance to the 'unity in diversity' of deliberative democracy. Hence I use the term *organic belonging* to describe 'unity in diversity', in order to emphasise two things. Firstly, experience of social solidarities (of being part of greater wholes) is an essential progenitor of a sense of personal ethics. It gives a grounding in everyday experience to the idea that human potentialities are to be used for the benefit of others as well as the self. Secondly, valuing both difference and commonness is not a contradictory stance, but requires a subtle moral sensitivity to what is of passing and what is of enduring value. On the one hand, cultural differences (such as gender, religious allegiance and nationality) are to be respected. Equally, they are not to be seen as the ultimate definers of personal identity and loyalty, legitimised by appeals to nature or divine command, and do not describe absolute boundaries of distinction. Hence, Fraser refers to 'an antiessentialist cultural politics of recognition' (1997: 187). On the other hand, there is something profound that connects human beings *qua* human beings, which is recognisable as deeply embedded in all and which calls forth an acknowledgement of fundamental equality. That is the contention of developmental democracy, and it is the very foundation of a democratic order.

According to the developmental model, democratic participation enhances the capacity to realise deeply embedded human potentialities. The tradition in which developmental democracy is founded encourages a particular stance towards modernity. It encourages a discourse which draws on particular concepts and ideas which include creativity, self-transcendence and reintegration of human capacities with the aim of challenging the dominance of instrumental rationality and the alienating character of the social order. Moreover, from a developmental perspective, people collectively – through state institutions and civil society – can, and are morally obliged to, create economic and social conditions which enable everyone to participate and work towards their human potential. People without sufficient food, employment, adequate housing, learning opportunities and educational stimulation are presented with greater obstacles to realising this potential. Developmental democracy, therefore, has a concern with social justice.

Leadership in the developmental model is concerned above all with aspiring to the common human good and working to create the conditions that give everyone a chance to fulfil their potential. Opportunities for leadership, in the sense of taking initiatives and seeking to influence others and the direction of society, its institutions and communities, are not the preserve of a small minority. They exist not only in the political domain but in a range of locations, such as local neighbourhoods, workplaces and voluntary associations, where developmental democracy sees that democratic involvement should be encouraged. In this regard, the model of developmental democracy overlaps with notions of deliberative and dialogic democracy (Giddens 1994).

This chapter has acknowledged the origins of modern democracy in the democratisation of access to religious knowledge and the idea that all people possess a creative capacity (even if it is confined and alienated in practice) to explore and work towards the good. However, many different conceptions of the form and scope that democracy might take have been put forward and debated over the centuries. Some of the key characteristics and principles of the main types of democratic theory have been synthesised and presented in this chapter in the form of four models of democracy, based on Stokes (2002), and their implications for leadership briefly outlined. In light of this discussion, it is suggested that the developmental model of democracy provides the most fertile and challenging theoretical framework for human and social development. The task now is to set out in greater detail, in the next chapter, a developmental conception of democratic practice in order to provide the necessary foundation to understanding democratic leadership.

Notes

1   Hill (1990: 207) is referring to D.P. Walker's book, *The Decline of Hell* (London: Routledge & Kegan Paul, 1964).
2   Griffiths emphasises the importance of heeding 'little stories (modest narratives) and local theories' (2003: 53).
3   From *A Dictionary of Famous Quotations* (1983: 376), compiled by Robin Hyman. London: Pan Books.
4   See Olssen et al. (2004: 260–61) on cosmopolitanism and communitarianism.

2 *A developmental conception of democratic practice*

Democratic practice takes its meaning and nature from the conception of democracy we hold. A broad conception implies that what it means to be active in a democratic society, organisation or group is rich, multi-dimensional and demanding, and that the institutional and cultural supports to democracy are geared to promoting this practice. Democratic leadership in the developmental model is concerned with distinct democratic principles which, in progressing through the models of democracy, have been introduced along the way. Brought together, these comprise the principles of the developmental conception of democracy and are summarised in Table 2.1.

Table 2.1: Principles of developmental democracy

Freedom	negative	freedom from constraint
	positive	freedom to be and act according to ones own direction
Equality		rule of equals by equals
Organic belonging	unity	belonging and interdependence within larger society and, ultimately, humanity
	in	which provides broader perspective for
	diversity	belonging and interdependence within ideals and identities that are integral to particular groups, cultures
Substantive liberty		freedom and enablement to realise human potentiality and become the goodly human

Democratic leadership also requires an idea of democratic practice which both analytically distinguishes and draws together its complementary and interacting dimensions (P.A. Woods 2003; 2004). Specifically, four rationalities, each with its distinctive focus, priorities and consequences, can be identified in a developmental conception of democratic practice (Figure 2.1), which build upon and complement the principles (Table 2.1). The

11

combination of rationalities expresses a view of human potentiality. Hence the conception fits a developmental model of democracy, as well as incorporating the valuable insights of the deliberative and others models.

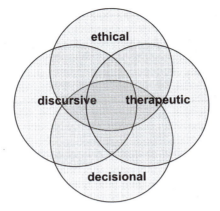

Figure 2.1: Rationalities of a developmental conception of democratic practice

Ethical rationality is concerned with supporting and enabling aspirations for truth, and the widest possible engagement of people in this. It is founded in the view that people as a group, community, organisation or larger society can approximate truths and improve those approximations. One of the functions of leadership in a democratic school is to 'engage people in processes that cause them to wrestle with issues and dilemmas that result in their constructing new knowledge about the issue or dilemma' (Reitzug and O'Hair 2002: 137). Moreover, this applies to questions of value and meaning as well as empirical statements. It is concerned with the search for veridical meaning, which comprises more than arbitrary assertion and has some purchase on what is truly and enduringly important. Two points should be emphasised about ethical rationality. Firstly, it is not just about *technical questions* – that is, questions concerning 'rational selection of instrumental alternatives' in a context where goals and values are given (Habermas 1974: 3). It is also about *practical questions* in which the choice or validity of values, norms and goals are open for questioning and determination (ibid). Secondly, it is not just about seeking answers at an abstract level. Technical and practical questions are answered through and in practical action.

A headteacher of a democratically managed school explains the importance of the collaborative approach in terms of finding the right way for this group and the best ideas.

There's no greater educator really than the influence of the group. Every group feels its way towards what's right for that group. I think sometimes very strong leadership can stop a group feeling its way outward and onward. For me, the entire movement outwards has got to be wholly felt within the group. It mustn't favour some people and not others, and I think there can be some odd distinctions about who has the best ideas. You don't have the best ideas because you're head, or because you've been here longer than anybody else. (Headteacher, Coombes School, quoted in Jeffrey and Woods 2003: 126)

In a similar fashion, an Australian school principal, talking about dispersed leadership, explains that there are 'so many people [at my school] with so much ability that I'm probably forced into recognizing that they have that and I'm not the only one who has all the answers and all the ability' (quoted in Lingard et al. 2003: 121). Surowiecki, in *The Wisdom of Crowds*, argues that this phenomenon – the ability of the group to find better answers to problems than lone individuals, however expert – is a general one: 'under the right circumstances, groups are remarkably intelligent, and are often smarter than the smartest people in them' (2004: xiii).

Ethical rationality raises the issue of who and what is counted as legitimate in contributing to the search for truth – namely, the *distribution of internal authority*. It is 'first amongst equals' amongst the democratic rationalities. This is because in the developmental conception the primary point of a democratic order is not solely to enable participation by all in the decisions that affect them, but to strive towards a way of living which is orientated towards the values that ultimately represent human progress and goodness. Ideas about what these values comprise, how to prioritise between their often conflicting implications and the best strategies for trying to realise them are contested and cannot be expressed as final, unquestionable truths. Still less can they be translated unproblematically into action. The lone, unchallenged leader cannot be relied upon to be the unerring compass to what is either technically or ethically right. Ethical rationality benefits from the engagement of many 'internal authorities' in forums which are, in this respect, the updated equivalent of the congregation intended to act as a check on individual absurdities, the importance of which was observed by Hill in the discussion of the origins of modern democracy (see Chapter 1).

This need to test and develop the ideas and claims of individuals reinforces the importance of embedding ethical rationality within the other democratic rationalities. Foremost amongst these is *decisional rationality*, which is about rights to participate in and affect collective, organisational decision-making. It concerns 'the conditions for the participation of citizens in all those decisions concerning issues which impinge upon and are important to them' (Held 1996: 310), including rights to select representatives. It is about who counts in decision making, and who is accountable and to whom. In short, this concerns the *distribution of externalised authority*; that is, the distribution of authority in external, collective decision making. And it cannot be taken for granted that entitlement to such authority only goes with formally demonstrable expertise. There is the simple point that being affected by decisions provides a case for participation. This is the stakeholder argument. And there is the point argued by Surowiecki that a variety of people with different ranges of expertise and information can contribute to good decision making. Despite our limitations as individuals – such as information deficiencies, lack of foresight, emotions which can bias judgements – 'when our imperfect judgements are aggregated in the right way, our collective intelligence is often excellent' (2004: xiv).

Decisional rationality also concerns enabling people to make choices and decisions that are rightfully theirs and to create and develop their own opinions, sense of identity and relationships. So it is about power and freedom from arbitrary and imposed rule by others and from the imposition of others' values, and enabling the exercise of individual liberty and social identities through diversity.

In order to take on the character of decisional rationality, democratic leadership needs to display several characteristics: *dispersal of leadership* throughout the organisation, which leaders work to recognise and enhance; *decisional rights*, which are not the same as consultation, but involve rights to vote, initiate or approve certain decisions and to hold power-holders to account (with sanctions available if they are judged to be wanting); *dampening of power differences*, whereby practical day-to-day power differences – between individuals, hierarchically organised posts or stakeholder groups (education professional, students, parents, and so on) – are not allowed to undermine effective participation. We shall see in Chapter 7 a number of examples where participation is undermined by, for example, 'invisible power' ingrained into everyday relationships.

Decisional rationality is summed up as genuine sharing of power, beyond consultation which involves simply expression of views. The idea of 'sharing power' encapsulates its essence and denotes a genuine participation in influencing the conditions in which one lives, and this may explain why it is a phrase that may appeal to students more than 'participation' or 'consultation':

> What [pupils] liked best was the idea of sharing power. This was a very vivid term that readily appealed to them. And it's certainly a graphic description, because without true power-sharing there is no democracy in a school. (Trafford 2003: 51)

Discursive rationality is about being actively engaged in debate and dialogue and is the day-to-day manifestation of deliberative democracy. It is about maximising the possibilities for 'the open debate of alternative interpretations and perspectives which recognizes their moral basis and [for seeking] a consensus on what would constitute appropriate action supported by good reason' (Sanderson 1999: 331). Its concern is *distribution of voice*. Giddens (1994) calls this 'dialogic democracy' and sees it extending social reflexivity and democratisation into four connected areas:

- personal life, such as family relations, including 'emotional democracy' (p. 119);

- social movements and self-help groups;

- organisations, including large private companies;

- the larger global order.

The school has its rightful place in this extended terrain of discursive rationality. As Trafford (2003) emphasises, alongside power sharing it is essential that school democracy involves the free exchange of ideas, which means seeking out and facilitating expression of views from teachers, students and parents.

Discursive rationality is integral to an active democracy, recognising that answers are not clear-cut, neither those of an ethical nor a scientific or technological nature. As Jorgensen explains

> The concept of dialogue not only means an acceptance of differences, but taking departure in these differences and considering them as fruitful for the joint enterprise. Dialogue mean '*dia logos*': reason flowing between us, reaching a new common reason which is greater than the individual reason we each possess. (2004: 121)

In other words, dialogue and deliberation are integral to ethical rationality, which is the aspiration to advance understanding and knowledge. And they are dependent on the principle of organic belonging which embraces unity and difference.

Therapeutic rationality concerns the creation of social cohesion and positive feelings of involvement through participation and shared leadership: in sum, the *distribution of esteem* (Chandler 2001). Whilst it is orientated to the interior well-being of the person, it recognises the intimate connection between external social relationships – their character, the symbols and messages conveyed by formal and informal social arrangements that encourage or discourage participation, the way differences in power and authority are made manifest – and the internal world of the person. For many students, especially the disaffected, as Riley found in a study in the North of England, schooling is a boring, hazardous, demeaning and 'joyless experience'; and they want schools to be more open and democratic so that they feel like partners in their own education (2004: 67). Participation has a positive emotional impact on teachers too, like the teacher in Lingard et al.'s (2003: 46) study who explained how much she appreciated having a say in what goes on in the classroom and the school.

The most radical and rounded form of democracy occurs where the four rationalities overlap. Their operation is intended to be developmental in the sense of the idealist tradition – a dynamic, social process of discovery, creative engagement, and movement from a limited perspective to wider, more worthy values. The rounded democratic actor represented by the four rationalities in combination is an idealisation of the creative actor who has broken through; that is, the individual who is able and enabled to be active in:

● the aspiration towards truth and enhanced understanding in all areas of life, including questions of meaning and values;

● making or contributing to decisions;

● discursive explorations of difference;

● giving and receiving support, self-confidence and respect.

It has been noted in passing that developmental democracy has a concern with social justice. A little more needs to be said about the distinction between democracy and social justice, however, as they can too easily be conflated. The respective centres of gravity of democracy (in its developmental conception) and social justice, and their interaction, are represented in Figure 2.2.

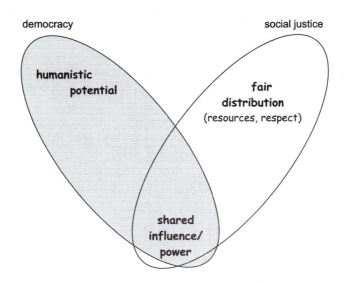

Figure 2.2: Respective centres of gravity of democracy and social justice

Democracy and democratic leadership are about who we are as social human beings, continually engaging in creative social action, influenced by and influencing others. This is what the developmental conception of democracy is most essentially about. Its centre of gravity is the flowering of the person – his or her positive attributes, capabilities and unfolding *humanistic potential* – in a social order in which they are actively and self-consciously engaged. The essential idea is the fundamental equality of worth amongst persons – ' ... the poorest he ... hath a life to live, as the greatest he'[1] – and their individual and shared capacity to generate ethical and meaningful knowledge.[2] From this derives the democratic imperative to share influence and power.

Social justice is about *fair distribution* – how resources, respect and opportunities can be justly distributed and social patterns of exploitation, domination and denigration eradicated. Cribb and Gewirtz's (2003) drawing together of three models of social justice (distributive, cultural and associational) is useful. Distributive justice is the absence of unjustified socio-economic inequalities, including exploitation, economic marginalisation (such as confinement to poorly paid or undesirable jobs) and deprivation (Fraser 1997: 13). I also include, as a component of distributive injustice, wide disparities in access to resources such as information and advice which enable people to locate and negotiate service provision.

Cultural justice is concerned with the absence of cultural domination, non-recognition and disrespect (Fraser 1997: 14). If the emphasis of cultural justice is respect for difference, the emphasis of democracy is unity as human beings. Hence, the principles of democracy include organic belonging, with a stress on the belonging, but these need to be reinforced by the respect which defines cultural justice.

Associational justice is the absence of 'patterns of association amongst individuals and amongst social groups which prevent some people from participating fully in decisions which affect the conditions within which they live and act' (Power and Gewirtz 2001: 41).

Each of these models of social justice affects the capacity for democracy and participation in democratic leadership. A conceptual overlap is evident through associational justice. The principle of equality – 'the rule of equals by equals' (Kelly 1995: 6) – gives democracy a direct interface with power differences.

Democracy and social justice both disrupt hierarchy. There are two directions from which this disruption travels. One is from a concern with interests – the inequities of distribution and access to material resources, social capital, cultural acceptance, status, and so on. This centres on fair distribution and is the crux of the concern of social justice.

Another direction is the positive and optimistic view of humanity, centring on humanistic potential, in which all have the spark of goodness and wisdom that enables and entitles everyone to have their say in the conduct of social life. This spark is confined neither to those in positions of authority, nor to the oppressed and powerless. The process of disseminating opportunities to share leadership, accordingly, turns 'the hierarchical pyramid upside down to discuss vision and values' (von Weltzien Hoivik 2002: 122).

The discussion to this point, in these opening two chapters, has set out an understanding of what the idea of democracy is about. In contrast to a narrow model of democracy, such as liberal minimalism, a broad notion has been advocated in the form of the conceptual components of a developmental conception of democratic practice. This lays a necessary foundation for considering the idea of democratic leadership. A further step is to place democratic leadership in the context of other concepts of leadership in education, which is the purpose of the next chapter.

Notes

1   Colonel Thomas Rainsborough, speaking in the Putney Debates during the English Civil War in 1647 (see Hill 1940).
2   Winstanley, a radical activist and writer on the Parliamentary side, urged people 'to leave off running after others for knowledge and comfort' and to allow spirit, reason, God to be 'the true teacher of everyone in their own inward experience' (Winstanley 1983 [1649]: 205). He goes on, emphasising that the learning that matters is not confined to the learned occupying the upper echelons of conventional social hierarchy: 'Many a poor, despised man and woman … [hath] more sweet peace, more true experience of the Father, and walks more righteously in the creation, in spirit and in truth, than those that call themselves teachers and zealous professors … [b]ecause these single-hearted ones are made to look into themselves, wherein they read the work of the whole creation and see that history seated in themselves' (ibid.).

3 *Models of leadership*

The reader might wonder whether there are not already sufficient conceptualisations of educational leadership. (One review of educational leadership listed more than 30 leadership theories – see Richmon and Allison 2003.) This point is addressed in two ways. Firstly, in this chapter, the notion of democratic leadership is placed in the context of other concepts of leadership. Secondly, in Chapter 4, the importance of democratic leadership is underlined and elaborated through discussion of its distinctive character in comparison with distributed leadership.

A typology of leadership concepts is shown in Figure 3.1. This is based on that of Bush and Glover (2003), and adds ethically transforming leadership and democratic leadership.[1] Some of these forms of leadership have a specific focus or highlight a particular aspect. Instructional leadership highlights the importance of leaders' influence on factors directly affecting student learning, for example, teaching methods, school climate or ethos (Leithwood and Duke 1999). Moral leadership concentrates attention on the values and ethics of leaders, so that authority and influence are to be derived from defensible conceptions of what is right or good (op. cit.).

The contingency theory of leadership focuses on leaders' responses to the unique organisational circumstances or problems that they face. Its particular insight is the recognition that 'the effects of one variable [the leader's traits, behaviours or context] are contingent on other variables' (Horner 2003: 28). Leithwood and Duke (1999) associate the contingent model of leadership with a craft or reflective concept of leadership, which stresses the importance of leaders' internal processes, and with Schon's (1991) concept of reflective practice or knowing-in-action. This reflective component is relevant to the developmental conception of democratic practice: the democratic leader is engaged in deliberation (discursive rationality), which complements and helps reflection, and in aspiring to 'find what is right' (ethical rationality) in given circumstances. Certain insights from research within the theoretical frame of contingency theory are helpful, such as observation of how 'followers' are categorised into 'in-groups' and 'out-groups' which then has implications for relations with formal leaders (Horner 2003: 29). Of itself, however. contingency theory

		Focus:
Instructional	→	influencing teaching and learning
Transformational	→	communicating a larger purpose and vision, increasing commitment and raising aspirations
Ethically transforming	→	ethically centred change, mutual raising of awareness and dispersed empowerment
Transactional	→	exchange relationships between leader and follower
Moral	→	values and ethics of the leader
Distributed	→	leadership as product of many people acting together, rather than any one individual
Democratic	→	shared governance by a multiplicity of free and equal leaders working together
Postmodern	→	multiple realities of diverse stakeholders, celebrating absence of common, unifying interpretation
Interpersonal	→	collaboration and interpersonal relationships
Contingent	→	adaptiveness to unique circumstances and problems of particular times and places

Figure 3.1: Concepts of leadership

does not provide a substantive theoretical framework of values and actions. Neither do the postmodern nor the interpersonal concepts of leadership.

Transformational leadership is an altogether more ambitious and expansive concept. It is about leading by communicating a larger purpose and energising and supporting followers so that they contribute more than that which is required to satisfy the transactional or contractual obligations of their position (Northouse 2004). It is associated with charismatic, visionary, cultural, and empowering leadership (Leithwood and Duke 1999). Transformational leadership is contrasted with transactional leadership, which 'is based on the exchange relationships between leader and follower' and comprises 'an exchange of services for various kinds of rewards that the leader controls' (Day et al. 2000: 14).

In the conception of transformational leadership which has been most influential in education, leadership is seen as comprising four dimensions (Gronn 1998: 201):

● inspirational influence – motivating subordinates through charisma;

● individualised consideration – treating subordinates according to their individual needs;

- intellectual stimulation – exercising influence on the thinking and imagination of subordinates;

- idealised influence – bringing about subordinates' identification with the leader's vision.

But this conception of transformational leadership has two key problems which will be discussed in turn in the next two sections. Firstly, it is too hierarchical and out of tune with contemporary social and organisational needs. Secondly, in the way it has evolved it has developed an ethical deficit.

Away with hierarchy: the promise of distributed leadership

Transformational leadership may be criticised as placing too much reliance on the top leader as an 'heroic' figure, encouraging manipulation of 'followers' and reinforcing dependence on a dominant echelon of leaders. Hence, in recent years, the importance of stimulating innovation and initiative throughout an organisational hierarchy has come to be recognised.

Behind this trend are pressures impinging on both private and public organisations, which are leading to changes in work relationships within and between organisations. The pressures on organisations include:

- the effects of global competition;

- technological changes, transforming information generation and communication;

- continued consumerisation of culture and ascendance of market ideology.

Hierarchy is seen by its critics as losing ground to networks and partnerships (P.A. Woods 2003). Greater emphasis is being placed on involving staff, engaging their commitment, encouraging dispersal of discretion and responsibility, and placing the highest value on continual learning, creativity and innovation. Private companies have increasingly come to see the importance of managing, generating and exploiting knowledge in order to survive and prosper in a globalised world. The most essential asset of the knowledge-based company – the intellectual capital of its employees – 'is best exploited, not by top-down direction, but by multi-level collaboration' (Bottery 2004: 9).

It is argued by Gratton that over the past decade or so 'it has become increasingly clear that through the forces of globalization, competition and more demanding customers, the structure of many companies has become flatter, less hierarchical, more fluid and virtual' (2004: xiii). People entering the workforce are increasingly characterised by the 'self-determination, autonomy and technical savvy' that demand respect and a more equal relationship within organisations (2004: xiv). Alongside this are rapid technological changes. Technology 'has the potential to recreate some of the closeness of ancient Greece, as it shrinks space and allows people to share information and knowledge rapidly and directly … [and] creates the widespread opportunity for individual excellence, autonomy and self-determination' (ibid.).

In his study of private sector organisations, Cheng (2004: 183) identifies a paradigmatic shift in organisational characteristics:

● from those at the top being the ones with most knowledge, to 'the frontline workers [being the ones] who need to possess knowledge and make decisions';

● from products manufactured according to plans handed down the hierarchy, to products 'designed and constructed at the front-line';

● an expectation, due to the changing nature of the market, that 'frontline workers … engage in just-in-time, on-demand learning of new knowledge and new skills appropriate to changing needs';

● blurred specialisation as staff are expected to be versatile and to integrate expertise in teams;

● work identity and success in the workplace influenced less by the qualifications staff possess and more by their qualities.

Amongst the implications are more working through project groups which 'function in teams by integration of expertise among members, with only a vague division of labour … [in which] members are expected to be versatile' (p. 181), and changed perceptions within these organisations of knowledge and learning.

Embedded in this globalised web of social and economic forces, public sector organisations experience their own particular pressures. Public services, including education, often find themselves subject to pressures to follow trends from the private sector. They have long been under pressure to prove themselves: in particular, to rise to the claim that private sector organisations are both more effective and more efficient, and to the challenge that the private sector has greater legitimacy and is less burdensome because companies are not dependent on 'imposed' taxation. Allied to this are relentless demands on public services to do more, for example, to serve populations which are living longer and have higher expectations and to embrace new possibilities in service provision opened up by technological advancements. New ways of working are being encouraged which blur traditional organisational boundaries. So, for example, recognition of the value of networks and partnerships has grown and there has been an explosion of interest in collaborative working between schools and other institutions and agencies (Woods et al. 2003; Glatter 2003), creating new challenges for educational leaders. Moreover, all of these changes are to be achieved in the context of perpetually squeezed finances: the pressure is on governments to keep public funds within limits, for fear of risking loss of competitiveness and capital investment and alienating middle-class voters. Hence reform of public services is in part 'a response to a growing belief that national economies increasingly face an in-built incapacity to finance the provision of public services' (Grimshaw et al. 2002: 476).

Part of the policy response has been to put public services under pressure to modernise their leadership (Woods and Woods 2004). In particular, increasing emphasis in both the public and private sectors is being placed on the idea of distributed leadership within organisations (Gronn 2002; O'Neill 2002; Bennett et al. 2003a; Woods et al. 2003). The idea is seductive and plausible. Its attractions lie particularly in its promise to enhance capacity and the organisations' ability to cope with and make a virtue of complexity.

The idea of distributed leadership acts as a conceptual counterweight to over-reliance on the 'heroic' leader. Leaders at the organisational apex are not unique sources of change and vision; nor do they act necessarily as single figures coaxing, persuading, inspiring or directing 'followers' towards better ways of working and the goal of organisational success. Distributed leadership thus gives an impetus to opening the boundaries of leadership beyond those in formal leadership positions.

What distributed leadership does most clearly is to draw attention to leadership as an emergent and dispersed property. Leadership arises from a variety of (planned and spontaneous) forms of co-ordination. Gronn, who has been the leading theorist on distributed leadership, identifies two types. There is *numerical* or *additive leadership*, which refers to 'the aggregated leadership behaviour of some, many or all of the members of an organisation or an organisational sub-unit', in which leadership is the outcome of distinct but interconnecting initiatives by a variety of people (2002: 3). The other type of distributed leadership is the most significant for Gronn. This is *concertive action*, in which there is an added dynamic from the process of individuals working together and the leadership collectively generated is more than the sum of its parts. Seen as concertive action, distributed leadership is not the agency of individuals, but is the result of 'structurally constrained conjoint agency, or the concertive labour performed by pluralities of interdependent organisation members' (p. 28). Transformational leadership, in the way it has evolved, overlooks the social dynamic that emerges from the combined agency of people taking and sharing initiatives and responding to and building on these proactively and creatively.

Ethically transforming leadership

The second problem with transformational leadership is the way it has, in its translation into business and education, lost an explicit ethical dimension of leadership. It is an abstracted conception of transformational leadership, divorced from a context of specified values, leading Day et al. (2000) to emphasise that transformational leadership needs to be explicitly values-led. Glenys Woods has drawn attention to this need and formulated a model of ethically transforming leadership which makes explicit the centrality of the ethical. As she urges, to 'get a full understanding of the ethical challenge which is integral to transformational leadership, it is essential to study Burns's original conceptualisation' (2003: 118).

The central concern of Burns's (1978) original conceptualisation of transformational leadership is with ethics and higher aspirations. The essential test of the Burnsian notion of leadership is whether it brings about change which constitutes progress towards achieving higher order values, such as liberty and justice. However, 'the current shaping of transformational leadership' in education 'supports existing power structures'; it is 'a "top-dog theory" that meets the needs of management' (Gunter 2001: 73). In other words, it is often used as an instrument of new managerialism. Hence, Bottery calls for a transformational leadership which does not simply serve 'centralised political and economic concerns' (2001: 201).

The model of ethically transforming leadership (Figure 3.2) formulated by Glenys Woods takes account of concerns about the original conception of transformational leadership. It is intended to incorporate both the best of Burns's conceptualisation – safeguarding its focus on ethically-centred change and the mutual raising of ethical aspirations and conduct – and the insights of a distributed view of leadership.

Ethically transforming leadership 'is essentially about people working together to raise one another's awareness towards higher ethical purposes' and aspiring to these as leaders deal with 'the practical issues and problems of everyday action' (G. J. Woods 2003: 122). Rather than sticking with 'a fixed binary classification of people into either leaders or followers', it involves 'a much more sophisticated interplay between individuals than implied by Burns's usage of the leader-follower binary' (ibid.). Moral insight is 'not confined to the person designated as leader', but, rather, 'spiritual resources and understanding are dispersed' (ibid.). This links with the origins of modern Western democracy in the democratisation of religious knowledge and access to truth. That original revolution brought to the fore the idea that capacity for understanding, critical deliberation and intuitive insights concerning ethics, meaning and human purpose are not the preserve of leaders at the apex of a fixed hierarchy. The capacity to examine what it is good and right to think and do in given circumstances, and translate this into

> *Ethically-centred change*, [which involves] working to higher order values (such as liberty, justice, equality, brotherhood, security, and order) and change which positively influences the well-being of those involved in and affected by that leadership (well-being being concerned with basic and higher human needs and inner resources, including the spiritual);
>
> *Mutual raising of ethical aspirations and conduct*, [which is about] going beyond narrow interests of the individual or the group towards the greater, unifying good of a common humanity (this includes raising the ethical aspirations and conduct of those in formal leadership positions as well as others);
>
> *Dispersed empowerment*, which means recognising that the capacity and responsibility for insight into and initiating ethically-centred change are shared, involve differing perspectives and are not confined to the designated leader(s), respecting the right of each individual to recognise his or her own true needs, and supporting the participation and valuing the voices of all.

Figure 3.2: Components of ethically transforming leadership (extract from G.J. Woods, 2003)

practical action – that is, a capability for benign creativity – is dispersed.

The concept of ethically transforming leadership is a progressive and worthwhile development of the original conception of transformational leadership. Giving prominence to dispersed empowerment helps to safeguard against transformational leadership being interpreted as justifying domineering, manipulative leadership.

However, dispersed empowerment needs elaboration and a more substantial theoretical underpinning which situates individuals engaged in leadership as social beings in historically specific cultural contexts and relationships. The individual focus of ethically transforming leadership is insufficient on its own. Whilst ethically transforming leadership and democratic leadership are connected by the priority they give to the ethical imperative, democratic leadership brings a social perspective derived from intellectual roots which deal with questions concerning the social evolution of modernity. It also focuses attention on the importance of social arrangements for deliberation and shared examination of the claims of formal leaders, as a check on 'individualist absurdities' (Hill 1975: 95). In other words, in matters of organisational leadership, trust cannot be given solely to an individualistic approach to ethical aspirations to truth and right action. Rather, individual commitment to ethically transforming leadership takes its place within the embedded and interlinking collective democratic rationalities: ethical, decisional, discursive and therapeutic.

Having placed the concept of democratic leadership in the context of other forms and ideas of educational leadership, the chapter which follows begins to delve further into that concept.

Notes

1   Distributed leadership is included rather than Bush and Glover's concept of participative leadership as distributed leadership is of key importance in considering democratic leadership. Bush and Glover include managerial leadership in their typology. It is not included here because, as Bush and Glover acknowledge, it represents a narrow focus that concentrates only on functions, tasks and behaviours.

4   *Why democratic leadership?*

In any age and social climate, there are some sweeping beliefs that seem to command respect as a kind of general rule – like a 'default' setting in a computer program; they are considered right unless their claim is somehow precisely negated. While democracy is not yet universally practiced, nor indeed uniformly accepted, in the general climate of world opinion, democratic governance has now achieved the status of being taken to be generally right. The ball is very much in the court of those who want to rubbish democracy to provide justification for that rejection.[1]

The significance of democratic leadership, and the reasons for attaching importance to it, are intimately bound up with its perceived meaning. In Chapter 1, it was argued that a broad conception of democracy was needed to underpin democratic leadership and, in Chapter 2, a developmental conception of democratic practice was outlined which founded democratic leadership in a substantive conception of the person as a social and creative being. This underpins the arguments in this chapter concerning the importance of democratic leadership as a concept in the field of leadership and management and as a way of leading schools.

In discussing these arguments, the chapter will elucidate further the substantive roots of the developmental conception of democratic leadership and practice. Such roots enable the notion and practice of democratic leadership to support leaders who take a critical stance to the status quo and want 'not only to challenge official models but put forward an alternative conceptualisation of leadership' (Gunter 2001: 121).

Instrumental reasons

Analytically it is possible to distinguish between two types of arguments for democratic leadership, though the distinction is not always hard and fast in practice. The first is *instrumental*. This envisages democratic leadership as a technique whose merit lies in the results it can be calculated to bring about, which have a value divorced from the technique itself. Instrumental reasons may be concerned with achieving organisational targets which can come to have an importance that overshadows deeper learning aims. In education there has been, internationally, a pervasive trend to increase regulatory frameworks and evaluate educational outcomes through inspections and measurement against performance targets. This reflects a concern with instrumental technical excellence and strengthens the structural force of instrumental rationality. The trend is reflected in assumptions about schooling and learning which have become more prevalent. From a critical perspective, Furman (2002: 7) identifies these assumptions as follows:

- The purpose of schools is instrumental, to serve national economic interests and supply the required workforce;

- The success of schools in this can be rationally determined by measurable student achievement;

- The individual's motivation for learning is instrumental; that is, to succeed on these measures of achievement and secure future financial prosperity;

- Teaching is a technical problem and teachers and schools can be held accountable for measurable student achievement.

It has been recognised, however, that neither teachers nor students are simple objects that can be driven to achieve goals by impersonal organisational frameworks and leadership and management techniques alone. Hence there is a marked interest in the emotional aspects of leadership (see, for example, Fullan 2001; Ginsberg and Davies 2003). In another sense, this is simply a re-realisation of something grasped by the idea of transformational leadership – that people have to *feel* commitment and a sense of direction and worth to participate in change. Greater recognition, accordingly, is being given to the importance of 'passion and purpose' (Goodson 2003: 67).

In addition to this – and despite the emphasis in educational policy on measurable achievement, giving rise to a performativity culture (Ball 2000) – there are signs of increased acknowledgement of the salience of other criteria, less amenable to comparative measurement, for assessing school education. In a pamphlet published by the UK's Department for Education and Skills, David Hargreaves argues that there is a

> growing recognition that in a knowledge-based economy more people need to be more creative and this will in itself require new approaches to teaching ... Without reducing the importance of basics, we must now aspire to nurture through education the qualities of creativity, innovateness and enterprise. (2003:4)

There is increased interest, too, in the importance and value of student voice and participation, even in relation to early years education (Mitchell and Wild 2004). Some countries, such as those in Scandinavia, have a policy history that has prioritised the promotion of democratic principles in education (though they are finding it necessary to respond to the challenges of globalised economic forces that put these principles under pressure; see Moos 2004). In the UK, in some ways the climate for student voice and participation has never been better. Klein writes:

> Student participation is in the ether and on the agenda. For the first time ever, legislation passed by Parliament has been put into place to ensure that children and young people's views are voiced, listened to and taken seriously in school. The Department for Education's guidance to schools on how to make themselves more democratic, interactive and accountable to students, hand in hand with Ofsted's [Office for Standards in Education's] new inspection remit to ensure that pupils are listened to, signals an exciting time for schools and a challenging one. These moves herald a potential shift in culture that brings children and young people into a power-sharing relationship with school managers, staff and governors. (2003: 1)

An observer might extrapolate and conclude that the trend in education is for it to become less instrumentally rational and more humanist in its orientation. But we should be cautious about making this leap. For example, a substantial part of what is occurring is a move from *simple instrumentalism* to *subtle instrumentalism*. Simple instrumentalism treats people (students and staff) as subjects who can be moulded and manoeuvred through direction and sanction, as means to organisational and economistic ends, and as organisational members whose worth and progress are to be measured through tests. Subtle instrumentalism retains the fundamental perspective of people as means to ends, but recognises that moulding, manoeuvring and assessing them requires a great deal more sensitivity to their emotions and motivations. It is a more finely tuned approach. However, if, as Fielding argues, the point is not to forge a 'reconfigured instrumentalism' (1999: 27), it is important to be wary of subtle instrumentalism as it still treats people as instruments rather than human beings with intrinsic value.

Nevertheless, intrinsic arguments should not be dismissed. It would be myopic to jettison all justifications framed in terms of 'outcomes' and the value of democratic leadership in coping with pragmatic problems and issues faced by policy-makers and practitioners. Some of these arguments concern interpretations of organisational trends in contemporary society, with schools being seen as institutions which do – or should – embrace these trends. Others are specifically focused on school education. Enmeshed in the arguments are threads of the rationale for distributed leadership. Highlighted here are some of the issues to which instrumental arguments for a more democratic style of leadership and practice in schools are addressed, namely:

- school improvement and effectiveness;

- engagement and self-esteem;

- organisational capacity;

- complexity and work intensification.

There are some indications that *school improvement and effectiveness* are associated with democratic and participatory styles of leadership. Harris and Chapman (2002) studied schools in challenging circumstances. They found that, although headteachers adopted autocratic approaches at times, in order to improve their schools the headteachers had deliberately chosen a form of leadership which empowered others to lead and had sought to distribute leadership activity throughout their schools. Studies in different national contexts have 'found that greater involvement in decision-making is characteristic of higher-producing schools' (Hallinger and Heck 1999: 181). With regard to student participation, and on the basis of studies conducted over a number of years, Ruddock and Flutter conclude that '[o]ur evidence suggests that a stronger focus on pupil participation [which includes consultation] … can enhance progress in learning' (2004: 11). However, a note of caution needs to be added. Demonstration of a simple connection is not proven. Much of the research does not show a direct connection and the impact may be variable amongst students (Airey at al. 2004). I will return to this point in Chapter 6.

There is perhaps stronger research evidence for a connection with student *engagement and self-esteem*. More democratic styles of teaching seem to enhance student's confidence and determination (Airey et al. 2004). Research findings tend to suggest that when given opportunities to be involved, students 'seem to find it fulfilling' (Flecknoe 2004: 411). Participation as peer mediators in conflict resolution enhances their self-esteem, sense of control and interpersonal skills (Clough and Holden 2002: 17). Ruddock and Flutter, on the basis of their research with students, conclude that 'opportunities for consultation and for enhanced participation in schools have a direct impact on pupils' engagement' (2004: 133). Where improvements in effectiveness and learning are found, then, part of the explanation may be increased engagement, interest and motivation, which reduces student disaffection (that is, student 'internal and external exiting'; see Gunter 2001: 137).

The positive impact of democratic involvement extends to school staff's engagement and self-esteem as well (Cheung and Cheng 2002). More generally, in the world of modern business, it is increasingly recognised that employee commitment cannot be taken for granted. With some support from research, it is argued that those 'who experience democracy are more engaged, committed and willing to give their potential to the organization' (Gratton 2004: 207).

Another potential contributory factor to enhanced effectiveness and learning is increased *organisational capacity*. This is one of the key rationales underpinning distributed leadership, which takes the view that leaders at the organisational apex are not unique sources of change and vision. Distributed leadership is seen as tapping the ideas, creativity, skills and energies which initiate and sustain change and which exist throughout an organisation, thus unleashing a greater capacity for organisational responsiveness and sustained improvement. The involvement of a variety of independently-minded people will, on the whole, lead to better decision making (Surowiecki 2004). Harris concludes that the central message from two studies of successful school headteachers was that the headteachers 'recognized the limitation of a singular leadership approach and saw their leadership role as being primarily concerned with empowering others to lead' (2004: 16). They 'gave their staff the confidence and responsibility to lead development and innovation' (op. cit.: 17). Another, more challenging way to put this is to accept 'the inherent weakness of leaders and work to inhibit and restrain this, rather than to assume it will not occur' (Grint 2005: 44). In other words, there is a need to recognise that formal leaders not only might make mistakes but, being human, *will do so*, and there is thus a requirement to nurture a culture and the institutional arrangements which support those outside, formal leadership roles, giving voice to disagreements and challenges and taking initiatives.

Democratic styles of leadership enable schools to cope better with *complexity and work intensification*. Sharing the burdens of leadership and teaching can help with increasing demands on time and effort, as well as with the numerous moral complexities facing contemporary school leaders. These are 'strong functional and instrumental arguments' for more democratic practice (Grace 1995: 203). Coping with complexity is another key rationale underpinning distributed leadership, which is seen as being better able to assimilate and manage the arrays of inputs and demands characteristic of information-rich societies. It promises a way of coping with the immense amount of information that is generated and circulated in modern societies and of maximising the chances of identifying the most relevant information and new knowledge and turning these to practical effect.

Commentators on the knowledge society conclude that managements of organisations in this new phase must 'differ radically from more "traditional" hierarchical ones' (Bottery 2004: 9). As Gronn points out, networked electronic communications technology 'facilitates the transcendence of previously insurmountable barriers of time, place and space by opening up entirely new possibilities for the performance of collaborative work' (2000: 334).

Intrinsic argument

However, the prime case for democratic leadership cannot be framed in terms of a better technical means to specified goals. It is not an 'add-in' to management techniques which will bring about 'improvement'. The second type of argument in favour of democratic leadership is *intrinsic*. This envisages democratic practice and leadership as something which has intrinsic worth, is integral to a good society and, in consequence, is intimately bound with education. Such a view is at the root of the developmental conception of democracy. The importance of considering democracy as of direct concern to school education is succinctly conveyed by Dewey when he highlights that it is not just something that happens in a nation's political institutions.

> Where democracy has fallen, it was too exclusively political in nature. It had not become part of the bone and blood of the people in daily conduct. Unless democratic habits of thought and action are part of the fibre of a people, political democracy is insecure. (Quoted in *Democracy in Education*, 1997, Vol 11, No 3, and requoted in Harber 1998: 1)

The point is re-inforced by Harber:

> If formal democratic institutions are to survive and to be sustainable in the long run, then they must be embedded in a civil society and political culture composed of both individuals and organisations which are permeated by values, skills and practices which are supportive of democracy. (1998: 1)

Schools and the society they inhabit are interlinked. There is a double-stranded connection:

● *From schools to society*: schools need to nurture tomorrow's democratic citizens;

● *From society to schools*: democratic society should, by its nature, enable schools to be democratic cultures inclusive of all who work in or have a stake in them.

The implication is that democratic leadership should be an integral part of education. Otherwise the ideal and the experience of education are at odds with each other. One of the 'powerful arguments' for more democratic school culture, as Grace (1995: 202) explains, is that failing to do this creates a contradiction between, on the one hand, the aim of education to aid students to become citizens of a democracy, and, on the other, actual experience which socialises them into non-democratic culture. 'Congruence' is needed between societal expectations and student experience (Harber 1998: 1). The same point extends to other stakeholders – school staff, parents and the community. Otherwise, they will experience a similar disjuncture between the ideals of the democratic society and practical experience at the local level.

Creativity, inclusion and reintegration

Intrinsic reasons are examined here through a comparison of distributed and democratic leadership, further developing the comparison in Woods (2004). Comparative profiles of distributed and democratic leadership are shown in Figure 4.1, which suggests where the democratic principles (see Table 2.1, Chapter 2) are principally threaded or brought to the fore in the democratic leadership profile.

Emergent and dispersed

Distributed and democratic leadership share a perspective on leadership as emergent and dispersed. Both see leadership as a social phenomenon which is not invariably or even usually reducible to the actions of a single person. What they point to is the additional effect of people working in concert with each other. Direction, impetus and energy arise from not free-standing initiatives, but the *circulation of initiative*.[2]

A theoretical grounding for this is given by activity theory (Engestrom 1999; 2000), which informs much of the work that addresses distributed leadership or is relevant to it (see, for example, Kets de Vries 1999; Karkkainen 2000; Spillane et al. 2001; Gronn 2002). Activity theory emphasises social life as a continuous flow of mediated activity; a process of continually changing relationships between technologies, nature, ideas, persons and communities. Action flows from one person to another in continuous circulation. One person can initiate change, with others following, contributing and adding to or altering it in various ways.

The engagement in this way of a multiplicity of leaders acts upon and alters the conditions, relationships and rules of that context. In other words, their actions as leaders act back on the structural properties which condition engagement. Both distributed and democratic leadership models bring to the surface, as a result, questions of who does and who ought to participate in leadership. Democratic leadership does this, however, in a richer conceptual and philosophical context.

Distributed leadership	Democratic leadership
• **emergent and dispersed** consists of additive and concertive action and is distinct from leadership by single leader	• **emergent and dispersed** mostly additive and concertive action, but can include leadership by accountable single leader
• **analytic concept** though often with implicit normative interpretations intellectual roots serve analytic emphasis, e.g. activity theory	• **analytic and normative concept** intellectual roots extend to broader theorisations of modernity (e.g. of alienation, instrumental rationality)
• **functional towards human capacities** in practice often emphasises leadership distribution according to the market/organisational value of people's discrete attributes	• **integrational towards human capacities** seeks recombination and engagement of all creative human capacities through overcoming of internal contradiction
• **inclusive, based on contingent status** boundaries of participation are circumscribed according to organisational needs, priorities, etc.	• **inclusive, based on human status** open boundaries of participation, based on equal valuing of all and equal distribution of externalised authority, voice, esteem and internal authority
• **instrumental autonomy** decisional participation is not defining feature; scope of concern with ethics is limited and pragmatic creative space, with its bivalent character of creative promise and unchecked challenge, judged in instrumental terms	• **inherent autonomy** freedom of expression and exploration through decisional and ethical rationalities in combination with discursive and therapeutic rationalities creative space embraced as necessary for human creativity
• **formally neutral** formally neutral towards dominant legitimacies of co-ordination (exchange and bureaucratic rational authority)	• **oppositional** opposed to arbitrary power differences and dominance of instrumental rationality embedded in exchange and rational authority

organic belonging

substantive liberty

equality

freedom

Figure 4.1: Comparative profiles of distributed and democratic leadership (showing democratic principles) (adapted from Woods, 2004)

Analytic and normative

Distributed leadership is best conceived as an analytical concept – that is, predominantly descriptive – which expresses some key ideas germane to leadership practice generalised across very different societies, organisations and groups. However, distributed leadership in itself is limited, in that it lacks the philosophical and theoretical depth of the developmental conception of democratic leadership. Democratic leadership grows from intellectual roots which address major issues in modernity and is analytic and normative. Essential to this is the creative character of humankind and a philosophical anthropology that provides the basis for an understanding of substantive liberty. These intellectual roots provide a set of concepts, founded in traditions of social critique, which enable critical engagement with contemporary challenges.

Democracy involves the breakthrough of the person as creative agent (see Chapter 1). But this is not a freedom solely for giving free rein to the pursuit of arbitrary personal preferences and private interests, as with liberal minimalism and consumer democracy. It is a positive liberty which takes up the challenges that arise with modernity. The developmental conception of democratic leadership rises to the profound challenges bound up in the powerful and entwined economic and instrumental rationalities of modernity, summarised in Figure 4.2. These are themes that infuse discussion of the arguments for democratic leadership.

- 'steel shell' of instrumental rationality
- pervasive concern with exchange value
- persistence of hierarchy and arbitrary power differences
- disenchantment of labour
- alienation

Figure 4.2: Challenges of modernity

The sociologist Max Weber expressed the first of these most starkly in addressing the question of what human type is encouraged by different social orders (Hennis 1988). This is central to understanding society and has fundamental implications for education. Weber is famous for his dour recognition of the pervasive sense of being trapped in the 'iron cage' – the *"steel shell" of instrumental rationality*[3] (Wells 2001) that came with the expanding bureau-capitalist order.

This person type *is* instrumentally rational in his or her very being, fated to exist in a disenchanted world without durable meaning. The only meanings in this rationalised modern world are subservient to the production and consumption dimensions of the market, with their perpetual drive to innovate and seek economic growth, or meanings driven by arbitrary preference, emotions and subjective attachment to belief systems. All meanings are arbitrary, without a potency secured in any enduring truth and hence lacking any content that can be taken to be veridical (even provisionally).

Despite arguments that bureaucracy is collapsing and that organisations in globalised capitalism are becoming more participatory and democratic (Cheng 2004; Gratton 2004), there persists a pervasive concern in the economic system with *exchange value*, which is about pursuit of calculable 'liquid' returns for expended work, rather than *use value*, which is about intrinsic worth. Complementary to this is a profound internalisation of instrumental rationality orientated to calculable returns and the achievement of organisational success. The spirit of capitalism specific to modern capitalism remains strong and, arguably, on the ascendant globally – that is, the 'rationalistic and anti-traditionalistic "spirit"' which involves 'the development of rational methodical practices in [the] conduct of life' (Weber 2001 [1910]: 120).

The trends underpinning the increased interest in distributed leadership seem to be consistent with a view that 'bureaucracy … is collapsing' (Cheng 2004: 183). But the *persistence of hierarchy and bureaucracy* should not be underplayed. Bureaucratic rational authority, expressed through hierarchical relationships, remains a significant way of legitimising social organisation, alongside markets and networks which extol the virtues of relationships based on exchange and bargaining (P.A. Woods 2003). Even though hierarchies may be flatter, there are still important formal differences in authority within organisations. Power differences are formed and sustained through complex and not necessarily visible circuits of power (Clegg 1989). A study of how the official promotion of collegiality fared in a school in Scotland, for example, concluded that teachers retained a strong sense of the prerogative of the hierarchy within and beyond the school to govern, even where they disagreed professionally with educational innovations (MacDonald 2004).

At the same time, a characteristic of modernity is that all legitimacies of power are open to question. Whether justified by tradition, charisma, legal-rational systems (Weber's three legitimacies), or even by democratic elections, everything is open to the question 'But why?'. The modern person is well aware that there are countless alternatives in the world and no arrangements are laid down by some universal requirement.

In this sense modernity reveals power. It reveals that some power is open and justified and some hidden and arbitrary. Power differences that are not subject to self-conscious legitimation by participants are arbitrary. Hence, hierarchies and power differences which have not been understood, agreed upon and accepted by those within them are expressions of *arbitrary power*.

The concern with emotional aspects of leadership and developing creativity and commitment to enterprise in education – subtle instrumentalism – is a response to two inherent problems in modern society. Firstly, the emotions of an older sense of vocation or calling have to be reawakened in new ways precisely because of pervasive instrumental rationality. A response to the *disenchantment of labour* is needed. Weber recognised that labour must be performed as if it is an absolute end in itself, namely, as a calling. His recognition that skilled and sophisticated labour cannot be motivated and sustained by the lure of wages alone (Weber 1971 [1930]:62) has its contemporary resonance in the attention given to emotions, relationships, hearts and souls in organisational studies (Fullan 2001: 52–5). This can be viewed in two ways:

- The *systemic* need is to get people to commit themselves to working in ways consistent with organisational requirements and powerful interests in the wider socio-economic system, and this requires overcoming calculated self-interest which leads people to minimise input and maximise returns for the individual;

- The *human* need is for a re-enchantment of labour, imbuing work with a sense of meaning, worth and validity rooted in enduring truths and values concerning human living.

How much of the emphasis on hearts and souls is made up of the instrumental use of emotion, with the aim of filling the gap left by a loss of enchantment in modern relationships – in other words, answering the systemic need? And how much comprises 'genuine relationships based on authenticity and care' (Lewin and Regine, quoted in Fullan 2001: 52), which answer the human need?

Secondly, there is *alienation*, in the sense that Marx intended – people being manoeuvred, distorted and confined by the constructs of human creativity (Fromm 1961). This means that economic relationships and the perceived needs of organisations shape the person, rather than vice versa. One of the contemporary forms of alienation is performativity culture (Ball 2000) which works in a similar way, fashioning school leaders, teachers and students so they become the kinds of people necessary to achieve organisational goals and succeed in terms of performance measures. Marx's elaboration of alienation points to questions of continuing relevance. Who may become most conscious of the dehumanisation built into the contemporary order and able to take initiatives that challenge that dehumanisation? Who leads change?

The great ideas of Weber and Marx seem to leave us in a fix. Weber diagnosed the problem, but he did not propose a therapy (Lowith 1993: 49). Marx had a therapy (proletarian revolution), but this turned out to be fatally flawed. Yet there are two reasons for looking for positive growth points from these intellectual roots.

Firstly, pointers to a therapy may be discerned in Weber's work. This hinges on the concept of *inner distance* and the expansion of its un-developed potential by Weber. Inner distance is the capacity for self-conscious adherence to ethical values in the face of daily pressures to conform to bureaucratic and market rationalities. This capacity suggests 'an unfettered self which tries to assert its individuality by affirming certain constant values in the face of the impersonal forces which increasingly dominate the modern world' (Schroeder 1991: 62). The capacity for inner distance enables people to exercise some degree of genuine interior author-ity (P.A. Woods 2003) and, hence, to participate as (more or less) free actors in a democracy.

Secondly, the positive side of recognising human alienation is that it is at the same time a recognition of human creativity. The latter provides the basis for giving substance to the idea of inner distance and of positive liberty (founded in some sense of organic belonging), which has something insightful and hopeful to say about the human potential on which devel-opmental democracy rests. The Hegelian roots of Marx's work have another flowering which helps us here. T.H. Green and the political philosophy of British Idealism that he founded, picking up the liberating potential of the religious and political revolution of the early modern era, proposed that the origin of an ethical sense resides not in external nature or circumstances, but in *human self-consciousness* which is simultaneously conscious of 'possible perfection and of actual imperfection' and of recognising in actions that the person 'is infinitely far from being what he has it in him to be' (Nettleship 1906: cxxxiv).

People are, to a greater or lesser extent, capable of orientating them-selves to that which is truly good and of enduring satisfaction to them as human beings aspiring to perfection. Both that which is truly good and its recognition emerge from and are properties of human self-consciousness. T.H. Green reformulates the idea of God from an external Being to an immanent characteristic of human consciousness. This aspect of con-sciousness has the potential to orientate people to truths that give meaning and direction beyond the mundane passions dominated by everyday sur-vival and individualised interests.[4] It is the basis for *benign creativity*.

The point here is that this understanding of the human condition and potential has consequences for our vision of education. Freire emphasises the dialectical movement that enables movement from alienation. Neither subjectivism (the idea that changing consciousness alone will change the world) nor objectivism (the idea that it is by changing the world that people's consciousness will change) are sufficient in themselves. We cannot change our thinking in isolation from what we do. As Freire puts it: ' ...

there is a unity between practice and theory in which both are constructed, shaped and reshaped in constant movement from practice to theory, then back to a new practice' (1985: 124). The implications for our understanding of knowledge and the curriculum I shall turn to in Chapter 5.

Integrational towards human capacities

Distributed leadership tends to be associated with a functional approach to human capacities, emphasising the valuing of expertise and the development of people who can most benefit the organisation, and developing people's potential in ways that contribute to organisational goals. Democratic leadership works for the integration of human capacities, giving some sense of what is involved in facilitating substantive liberty. People's capacity for overcoming alienation, as opposed to arbitrary defiance of given cultural values and norms, needs to be understood and appreciated.

As we have seen, emotions are capable of being used as a means of engaging people to organisational goals and interests in order to re-enchant labour artificially. However, as Barbalet (2001) points out emotions are incapable of being bought and possessed entirely as a product or commodity. Conscience and honour, for example, retain their 'pre-commodified' quality because they continue to be possessed by those who have them (op. cit.: 182). Fevre argues for a 'recombinant sensibility' (2000: 215) which involves the enhanced valorisation and use of human capacities that are undervalued. A cognitively dominated instrumentalism makes sense of the world in only a limited fashion. Yet people have suppressed capacities for sense making in particular emotions, like love, that help us to explain, understand and orientate ourselves to the world.

But the philosophical anthropology of democracy underpinning democratic leadership does more than recognise this. Firstly, it distinguishes within the affective domain between feelings concerned with matters of the highest worth and mundane passions dominated by everyday survival and individualised interests. The former are *navigational feelings* that orientate us to what should be counted as true and of worth (Woods 2004). An understanding of social justice, for example, derives, at least in part, from a primitive sense of what is right. The desire for justice

is something that is found in the youngest of children. 'It's not fair!' is a familiar cry. Even if the sentiment is not expressed in words, it is deeply felt. Adults vividly remember those times in their childhood when they were treated unfairly. Young people between childhood and adulthood crave respect, and see that it must be reciprocal ... (Griffiths 2003: 127)

Navigational feelings are of crucial importance in raising the affective domain beyond arbitrary passions and self-interest. Such a human capacity is what T.H. Green was pointing towards in the idea of a moral orientation, inherent as a potential in the individual, to the '"true good" ... which provides abiding satisfaction' (Boucher and Vincent 2000: 38). The individual ego has the inherent potential to become aware that 'a more perfect form of existence is possible for itself' (Green 1886: 326), a 'higher self that is not satisfied by the objects which yet [the person] deliberately pursues' (op. cit.: 324), and to be 'moved to action by that consciousness' (op. cit.: 326).

This area of inner ethical potential has been explored within the field of psychology by Donaldson (1993) in her studies of value-sensing. I have elaborated the related concept of values-intuition as a potential feature of social action (Woods 2001). In his sociological analysis of the genesis of values, Joas points to the importance of the living foundation of values in 'experiences of ... self-transcendence' (2000: 164). The self's consciousness of life's limitations and mortality itself engenders a sense of ideals, superordinate values and eternity, and the felt importance and personal empowerment of surrendering the ego to some kind of 'ideal authority' (op. cit.: 81)[5].

Research suggests that spiritual experiences in contemporary times are a major source for navigational feelings. Such experiences have been shown to be influential for the professional life and educational conduct of school leaders (G.J. Woods 2003). It is important to be tentative and self-critical about these as sources of knowledge – in other words, to apply a critical epistemology to their claims (see Chapter 5). However, navigational feelings are significant contributors to veridical meanings which point to enduring values and offer practical orientation to leaders.

Secondly, alienation is not a static state but holds the potential for change as a process. Instrumental rationality and navigational feelings are contradictory elements within the person because of the dominating character of the former. Transcending alienation involves awareness and practical change. The spirit of Marx's dialectical analysis of alienation is about identifying and yielding the good suppressed in the present,[6] revealed through the latter's contradictions, in order to make the best of this fundamental tension in the social conditions in which people find themselves. The 'steel shell' of instrumentality suppresses the full potential of the affective domain of the self. Democratic rationalities are often overwhelmed by the powerful instrumental rationality integral to exchange and rational authority. Democratic leadership in pursuing the educational aim of enabling all to become democratic citizens seeks to overcome the contradiction between two forces:

* *the constraints of today's reality* – the social dominance of instrumental rationality, characteristic of a social order driven by arbitrary meaning;

and

● *human potential* – navigational feelings, contributory to veridical meanings pointing to enduring truths.

Heightened consciousness of powerful instrumental rationality serves to
sharpen over time appreciation of the affective domain and its significance
for our humanity. To put it another way, consciousness of this dehumanisation is embedded in each person by virtue of the character of the affective domain. Human potentialities 'when they are suppressed and opposed
will in time rebel and demand an opportunity for manifestation' (Dewey,
quoted in Henderson 1999: 4). Further, those towards the bottom of the
hierarchy are often especially capable – potentially – of sensitivity to, and
awareness of, suffering brought about by impersonal forces.

Two processes are necessary for change. Firstly, pre-commodified navigational feelings, which are the basis of inner distance from instrumental
rationality, need to be recognised and developed. Such feelings include positive sentiments towards the realisation of second-order values, like honesty
and fair treatment, and negative feelings towards their opposite. They
include more profound affective responses to events, people or social orders
that give expression to higher, first-order values, such as compassion,
liberty and justice. An example would be love for a person who embodies,
through their character and actions, compassion and selflessness in the
pursuit of justice and freedom for others.

Intense and profound negative sentiments to actions and people that
represent extremes of the denial of higher values also signal the existence
of these values. An intense affective response giving rise to a sense of viola-
tion of such higher values is itself a sign that they do indeed exist. Hence,
the sociologist Peter Berger argues that one of the signs of principles and
ideals that transcend material and mundane interests is people's sense of
being 'fundamentally outraged' at certain acts (1973: 84), such as the Holo-
caust, which 'seem to violate a fundamental awareness of the constitution
of our humanity' (p. 85).

Secondly, moving beyond the recognition and development of such
navigational feelings, there needs to be a recombination of emotional
senses and instrumental rationality which transforms the latter into an analytical and organising capability complementary to navigational feelings.

The capacity to assert ethical values in the face of contemporary social
and economic forces is an essential feature of education which aims to lift
people towards their human potential. An integral part of democratic leadership is creating the conditions which are conducive to the reintegration
of human capacities through the development, application and recombination of affective capacities with a complementary analytical rationality.
Adoption of the concept of democratic leadership in school contexts

encourages an educational approach which poses and addresses some of the deepest questions about human beings and what constitutes valued learning.

Inclusive, based on human status

Whilst distributed leadership gives an impetus to the opening of the boundaries of leadership, and so includes more people in leadership, this is a conditioned inclusivity. Distributed leadership is more often about inclusivity based on contingent status. Much of the discourse surrounding distributed leadership places an emphasis on distribution of leadership according to the market or an organisational value of people's expertise, skills and motivation. Boundaries of participation are, therefore, circumscribed according to organisational needs and priorities. Boundaries may be drawn, by imposition or negotiation, at different points within an organisation, and may or may not include groups outside it. In the case of schools, whilst teacher leadership is a matter for study and discussion (see, for example, Leithwood and Jantzi 2000), less prominent in the field of leadership is a focus on non-teaching staff, students and parents.

Democracy adds to the emergent character of distributed leadership the idea that everyone, by virtue of their human status, should be an active participant in democratic practice. Democratic leadership champions inclusion based on human status. This is the consequence of a sense of common humanity and a fundamental valuing of each person – the centre of gravity for democracy. The state of *communitas*, or the free space with its diminished social distinctions and statuses which we shall come to in Chapter 8, helps to remind people of 'an essential and generic human bond, without which there could be *no* society' (Turner 1969: 97; original emphasis). This bond, which underpins a sense of a common humanity and has implications for how we treat and include each other, is integral to democratic leadership. From this perspective, the human status of those within, and associated with, an organisation is the ultimate touchstone determining rights to participate. Pragmatic matters will, nevertheless, have a bearing on the degree and nature of involvement by different groups (discussed further in Chapter 11).

Inherent autonomy

Distributed leadership is not about the valuing of personal autonomy per se, but is more accurately described as being concerned with instrumental autonomy. Although leadership may be distributed, it does not necessarily imply an absence of direction and constraint cascading down a hierarchy. Studies indicate how some forms of distributed leadership work with strong leadership from senior leaders, and are bound by aims and values set by superior levels within and beyond the organisation (see, for example, Graetz 2000; Harris and Chapman 2002). In other words, distributed leadership varies in the balance between control and the autonomy which participants are allowed or enabled to exercise (Woods et al. 2004). Often limits will be set, by over-arching organisational values and goals, to the scope for dispersed initiative, that is, the terrain of issues and organisational activities open to independent initiative. In education these have been increasingly set by central regulation, performance targets and inter-institutional comparisons aimed at producing skills and attitudes required for competitive and globally-orientated market economies (Apple 2000; Gewirtz 2000; Bottery 2001). Participation by team working is often focused on finding creative and effective ways of overcoming specific problems or reaching pre-defined goals.[7]

Democratic leadership values autonomy of the person as an inherent good, which is connected with the principle of freedom. It also provides at least part of the answer to the educational question that addresses Weber's fundamental cultural question. What type of person is the educational social order that makes up the school meant to encourage? The answer embedded in the developmental conception of democratic leadership is the truly creative agent, capable of dealing with the pressures of modernity and moving towards the aim of 'self-conscious self-determination', which is the antithesis of alienation.[8] This person can recognise and use the potential of inner distance. For students, this means helping them to develop 'a reasoned and responsible autonomy' and 'the task for schools is to help young people exercise power over their own lives both in school and as an investment for the future' (Ruddock and Flutter 2004: 129). For staff, it means expressing, through their engagement in shared leadership, a commitment to substantive values of democracy and social justice, a capacity for independence and a 'critical consciousness' of issues beyond the school, which include the global, social and personal effects of capitalism in its contemporary phase (Bottery 2002: 173).

The answer to the cultural question about the type of person meant to be encouraged, is not dependent on the degree to which a person contributes to functional criteria laid down by the school or state. The answer is guided by the multi-dimensional practice which engages human potentialities: human potential to integrate ethical, decisional, discursive and therapeutic rationalities in concert with others. Democratic leadership values creative space as necessary for human creativity and flourishing, not merely as a means to more effectively achieving organisational goals.

Oppositional

Distributed leadership is formally neutral towards issues of private or public ownership, markets or democratic control, and other such issues. However, it lends itself to being uncritically harnessed for the pursuit of goals and values which are contestable and in contention with humanist values of education. As a result, in its practical manifestations there are often normative tendencies or implicit values assumptions implicated in distributed leadership.

Democratic leadership, by its nature, is involved in confronting the major challenges inherent in modernity. Democratic leadership recognises the need for an oppositional stance to the dominance of instrumental rationality and the alienating character of the social order. Hence, it involves ideas and action which are in tension with market servitism (Woods 2002), instrumental rationality and the separation and evaluation of people's capacities according to market and functional criteria. It exists in permanent tension with relationships and power differences that are legitimated by self-interested exchange (typically the market) or by rational authority (modern bureaucracy) (P.A. Woods 2003).

Democratic leadership has two sides. One side looks forward to enabling the positive potential of people – creative autonomy and reintegration of human capacities – whilst the other side has to contend with the dominating forces of modernity (see Figure 4.2). It is that duality, or the positive enabling of creative potential together with a recognition of 'hard' realities, which makes democratic leadership relevant to education in the context of a global capitalist economic order (Bottery 2001). It takes to task the 'neoliberal view of the performing school [which] requires teachers and students to be followers, but to feel good about it ... ' (Gunter 2001: 122).

Because developmental democracy is not just about the external organisational order, but integral to it is a respect for each individual and his or her human potential, democratisation engages the whole person. Hence, it is concerned not only with the integration of human capacities (as has been discussed), but has in common with Nemiroff's (1992) notion of critical humanism a concern to address both the social context of modernity and the internal world of idiosyncrasies, imagination and personal feelings.

Critical humanism combines the focus of critical pedagogy on social issues, such as the emancipation of oppressed groups, with a recognition and respect for the 'often eccentric or individual psychological dimensions' (op. cit.: 57). Each person's expertise concerning their own lives – their internal authority (P.A. Woods 2003) – is recognised. Critical humanism 'starts with individual feelings, which are brought into contact with external factors that then contribute to the form these feelings take' and help empower people to understand how 'lives are mediated and controlled by those social definitions and institutions' which serve dominant groups and interests (Nemiroff 1992: 89).

The principles of developmental democracy, with their themes of liberty, equality and belonging, demand the spanning of the social and personal. Developmental democracy also adds to this the potential for navigational feelings which enable the internal affective dimension to orientate the person to action and values that ultimately represent human progress and goodness.

This chapter has spent some time articulating the reasons for attaching importance to democratic leadership in education and in doing this has elaborated the intellectual roots and ideas that contribute to a developmental conception of democratic leadership. The relevance of instrumental reasons for advocating democratic leadership has been acknowledged. Greatest attention, however, has been given to instrinsic arguments, explored through a comparison with distributed leadership and summarised in Figure 4.1.

The next task is to consider what epistemological implications are associated with democracy, the subject of the following chapter. This will complete the conceptual exploration of the developmental conception of democratic leadership. It will then be possible to examine the connection between democratic leadership and learning (in Chapter 6), before discussing (in Chapters 8 to 10) characteristics and issues that need attention in creating and sustaining democratic leadership.

Notes

1   Sen (1999: 5).
2   There are links here with the sociological theory of analytical dualism (Archer 1995) which advocates a critical realist approach emphasising institutional, cultural and social phenomena as emergent properties of social life. (See also Gronn 2000; Woods 2000).
3   The usual translation of Weber's original text as the 'iron cage' of the bureau-capitalist order is better rendered in English as the 'steel shell' (Wells 2001). What confines people is not an external 'cage', but something much more insidious: a characteristic which has become part of the person (as a shell is an organic part of an animal) and which is forged (like steel) by human beings in modern society.
4   Human consciousness contains within it, in the Idealist interpretation, a reproduction of an eternal mind or self-consciousness and so the good life has a metaphysical meaning far beyond the mundane passions of this world. See Nettleship (1906: cxxxiii) and also Boucher and Vincent (2000: 38).
5   Here Joas is expounding the sociologist Simmel's explanation of self-transcendence, though he does not embrace Simmel's theorising on this in its entirety.

6   See Marx (1973: 161–2, 881).
7   Not all leaders working in concert and investigated as cases of distributed leadership are driven purely by instrumental motives. See, for example, Gronn (1999) and Gronn and Hamilton (2004). However, the discourse of distributed leadership tends to situate such leadership as an instrument of given organisational and economistic goals.
8   *Oxford Companion to Philosophy*, Oxford University Press, 1995 (from website, www.xrefer.com/entry/552724). See also Meszaros's (1970: 162–8) discussion of Marx's notion of 'self-mediation'.

5 *An open approach to knowledge*

The intimate connection between democracy and creative human potential is the foundation of the developmental conception of democracy. The presupposition of this conception is that people are capable, individually and collectively, of creative social action. So, with regard to literacy for example, Freire argues:

> If learning to read and write is to constitute an act of knowing, the learners must assume from the beginning the role of creative subjects. (1985: 49)

As suggested in the previous chapter, to overcome alienation a dialectical movement is needed between subjectivism (changing consciousness) and objectivism (changing the social and material context in which we live). Critical capabilities are essential to this. Democratic society needs to 'seek through education to provide pupils with the skills necessary to see their problems in a reflexive perspective and thus enable them to gain some control over their own destinies' (Kelly 1995: 81). Hence literacy – to continue with this example – is seen not as a technical accomplishment, but is inherently part of learning as a human being to reflect on and act in the world. True literacy is 'associated with the right of self-expression and world-expression, of creating and re-creating, of deciding and choosing and ultimately *participating in society's historical process*' (op. cit.: 50; emphasis added).

This reflects a notion of substantive liberty to which education helps the learner aspire. A similar notion is found in the second of two forms of socialisation distinguished by the Norwegian philosopher, Hellesnes (Moos 2004). The first – *conditioning socialisation* – 'reduces humans to objects for political processes which they do not recognize as political', rendering them suitable for direction and control (Hellesnes 1976: 18, quoted in Moos 2004: 7). This is antithetical to democratic education. The second – *educational socialisation* – emancipates people so that they are able to be competent and autonomous political actors. This is socialisation which enables the student to engage creatively in shaping the structures (institutional, cultural and social) that form the context of his or her life. Its educational aim is 'to develop the kind of knowledge of the world which allows a sense of its transformability, and to develop the skills which enable people to participate in such change' (Jones with Franks 1999: 47). Promoting a curriculum that aims to do this is a central task of democratic leadership.

Implicated in this task is a view of how knowledge is generated and circulated, and how we, as creative mediators of culture, construct understandings of the world. Hence, democracy carries with it a certain understanding of how we as human beings are able to know the world. It has philosophical underpinnings that have epistemological implications. People are creators of knowledge rather than passive recipients of revealed or already-discovered knowledge.

A typology of perspectives of knowledge, which is a radically simplified representation of a complex field of philosophy, is shown in Table 5.1. It has the virtue of throwing into sharp relief certain key, contrasting features of epistemology – namely, the view taken of knowledge and of the social dynamic underpinning the approach to it, and the perspective taken on truth and what constitutes the basic aim of education.

Table 5.1: Perspectives on knowledge

	Differences in approach to:			
	Knowledge	Social dynamic underpinning knowledge	Truth	Aim of education
Critical	tentative	unity in difference	aspired to	autonomous discovery
Rationalist	certain	unity	known	assimilation
Post-modern	ephemeral	difference	abandoned	self-construction

The critical perspective on knowledge has its roots in empiricism where the test of validity is not against a text, theory or an authority, but against experience and critical examination. In this perspective nothing can be finally proven (Hume 1969 [1739/40]). But the critical perspective on knowledge does not equate with a simple empiricism that believes in unmediated observation of 'facts'. It represents more of a Popperian stance in which our ideas and theories of the world are continually tested against experience and data (Popper 1979). Knowledge and understanding are tentative. There is, therefore, room for difference and diverse perspectives and points of view and new hypotheses. Indeed, that is necessary and encouraged. Nevertheless, the aspiration is towards truths and, to this end, the continual improvement of understanding. In difference, we are also seeking to expand the knowledge which unites us; that is, to enhance our shared comprehension of and insight into our selves and the world we inhabit. Such understanding is advanced through critique. Hence, it is vital that people are enabled to develop and apply their critical faculties, which include their rational capability and their affective capacity for navigational feelings, so that they can independently, individually and with others, challenge and discover.

Kelly has marshalled well the arguments for the special relationship between democracy and what I term here the critical perspective on knowledge. He emphasises that for students in a democratic education the 'central task is to learn to question and challenge all the "knowledge" they are presented with' (1995: 92). This kind of development

> cannot be brought about by the assimilation of knowledge; it can only be attained by using, testing and developing knowledge in the process of solving real problems – in short, by addressing a problem, framing a hypothetical solution and then testing that hypothesis to see if it 'works'. (1995: 92)

Indeed, for Kelly, 'to be opposed to this form of education is to be opposed to democracy itself' (p. 93). Democracy 'implies a view of knowledge as uncertain, tentative, provisional, evolutionary and subject to constant challenge, questioning and possible modification' (p. 117). A primary school teacher participating in research undertaken by Jeffrey articulates this. She describes her teaching as modelling 'the kind of thought processes and questioning of the knowledge' she wants to teach, and continues:

> In fact I was doing that in Art this afternoon. OK, I was asking for their response, but I was responding as well, as a person not a teacher. When I am working, I am always conscious of modelling my learning. It is being able to learn about learning as well. As a teacher, I am quite conscious of wanting to be a learning model. I am not the holder of knowledge that they have to unlock. (Carol, a Year 6 teacher, quoted in Jeffrey 2003: 496)

A post-modernist perspective on knowledge takes the critical approach still further. The idea of post-modernism can be taken to mean different things (Kelly 1995). But I take the view that, in essence, it is the stretching of modernism, and in particular the critical perspective of knowledge, to its most extreme position. So, knowledge does not really exist but is the passing, transitory and ephemeral beliefs of the moment. Difference and diversity are celebrated. Most crucially the very idea of truth is set aside and considered an illusion to be left behind. The educational aim is for the person to be able to build a sense of identity and to change identities.

I should acknowledge here that the Foucauldian thesis which challenges traditional commitments to truth has a point, and one which encourages a proper, critical alertness to truth claims. It argues that what is taken to comprise truth at any point in time is the outcome of power relations embedded in the status quo. Truth is an effect of power. In light of this, Giroux, for example, argues that intellectual practice should be tied to 'an alternative and emancipatory politics of truth' and 'be grounded in forms of moral and ethical discourse and action that address the suffering and struggles of the oppressed' (1989: 212). However, this statement – if it is meant to invite the critical reader to agree – must rest on the idea that a better life for those who suffer and are oppressed (regardless of whether we are members of this group of people or stand in a different relationship to them) is to be valued and that it makes sense (conceptually and empirically) to refer to 'suffering', the 'oppressed' and 'struggles'.

There are ideas about the world and values implicit in the statement, which comprise universal claims of truth and meaning. I do not argue with the statement. My point is that it is not reflective of a post-modernist epistemological stance; rather, it is making claims to validity which are compatible with a critical perspective on knowledge and, like other propositions and claims to knowledge, ought to be approached with a questioning mind and be subject to continual challenge and possible modification. The problem with post-modernism as an epistemological stance is that it takes the uncertainty of the critical perspective on knowledge and makes it the final word on the human condition. It purports to leave behind the difficult job of grappling with how to improve our understanding of reality by abandoning the very idea of truth.

The rationalist perspective is the epistemology which stands in sharpest contrast to the critical perspective and, in isolation, is incompatible with democracy. This views certain truths as known. The consequent need is to ensure that everyone is enabled to understand what those truths are. After all, it is axiomatic that it is sensible and good to accept that which is true. The source of knowledge may be scientific discovery and theoretical analysis, or revelatory pronouncements from prophets, or truths discoverable in sacred texts. The aims that follow from this certainty are to transmit these known truths so that all can assimilate them and to bring everyone to a unity of understanding around them.

Kelly's concern that a rationalist perspective on knowledge is incompatible with democratic education has some force. Religious schooling, for example, which inducts children into a fixed belief system that is presented as unchallengeable truth seems at odds with a democratic society in which respect for other versions of truth is a fundamental principle. Even more threatening to democracy are instances where the beliefs of one group deliberately demonise others in the same society and justify prejudice and even violence.

However, it would be going too far to eliminate from education any rationalist approach to knowledge. Whilst education is a process that involves discovery and challenge on the part of learners (the critical perspective on knowledge), it also entails, as part of that process, transmission and assimilation. Learning, outside and inside school, involves absorbing ideas about the world which give some sense of knowing and contribute to a sense of identity. Following assimilation, the learner may become conscious and, in time, reflexive and critical of this. In the realm of values, the source of the learning and identity building may be a faith context for some, whilst for others a secular or non-religious one, or a strongly politicised worldview.

In practice, as a sense of knowing starts to take hold, it is learnt, to a degree, as knowledge emergent from a rationalist epistemology. Or, perhaps, it is taken in *as if* the knowledge is rationalist. What I mean by this assertion is that the perceived or explained validity of learnt ideas has a quality of *giveness* – whether that be through its derivation from a text, a theory, or an authority (such as the teacher). At the point of assimilation, it is not necessarily, or appears not to be, open to challenge. Such knowledge contributes to a person's conjectural maps that orientate them to the world and enable them to chart their actions (Woods 2000).[1]

So, for example, knowledge about a particular novel or poem, and, say, its place and meaning in the historical context of writing, enables the student to begin engaging with that writing. Or, in order to engage with a problem – in science or in practical curriculum areas – some understanding of relevant principles and information is a pre-requisite. Before engagement, 'threshold knowledges' (Lingard et al. 2003: 39) are needed. In the arena of values, philosophy and religious belief, people first develop by absorbing ideas and cultures that provide interpretations of who we are and of social life and which signal what value and importance aspects of the world have. People cannot tackle intellectual, artistic and practical challenges, and grow, as *tabla rasa*. Rather, they take in, build, revise and refine, or replace, conjectural maps. Students '*need* specific knowledge that can be used to solve (what to them) are important problems' (Knight 2001: 253).

This movement between rationalist and critical approaches in the practical engagement with knowledge occurs and recurs in periods of varying length. For example, it may characterise a process over several years, or one which takes place in the classroom. It can be seen in the six stages experienced by a headteacher with the class for which she was also the teacher (see Figure 5.1).

Stage 1: delivering the curriculum. Fitting with the traditional role of the teacher as passing on curricular content from one who knows to those who don't.

Stage 2: beginning to discuss with pupils the purposes and objectives of what they are learning. What is the objective of your learning?

Stage 3: involving pupils in considering and writing down indicators by which to measure their achievement. How will you know when you have learned something?

Stage 4: involving pupils in assessing their own and others' work. How good is this piece of work? What criteria can be used to judge it?

Stage 5: pupils becoming determiners of learning. They make decisions about the when, how and what of classroom learning. What is the best way to do this?

Stage 6: collaborating with pupils as learning partners. What shall we do together to improve the conditions, processes and evaluation of our learning?

Figure 5.1: Stages of teaching (extract from MacBeath 2004: 43–44)

Assimilated knowledge has something of the character of Winnicott's (1971: 3–14) transitional phenomena which are necessary for development but which people move beyond, recognising the illusions inherent in them. However, I would not suggest that all the components of received knowledge are discarded and ascribed as illusion. Some stand the test of time, perhaps being recast in the evolving interpretative understanding of the learner.

In a democracy the starting points for learning cannot be prescribed in any absolute sense. Respect for the diversity of cultural contexts is part and parcel of the democratic principle of organic belonging. Where educational diversity involves schools of different philosophies or religious orientations, there are, however, principles that apply in a democratic society. What the democratic community in order to be democratic wants to encourage amongst diverse cultures is:

- respect for the creative potential of each person, including young people, and that includes both their critical, rational capability and their affective capacity for navigational feelings (the foundational creative agency of democracy); and

- respect for other cultures within society (cultural justice).

This means that all, to a degree, embrace a critical perspective on knowledge, which involves people applying their analytical faculties to challenge and discover for themselves.

A key question that modernity and the critical perspective on knowledge cannot avoid is: If everything is uncertain, how do we take action? People need to act as if certain things are true. This includes scientific propositions, such as inference of cause and effect, and the assumptions involved in day-to-day interactions. Without some practical sense of certainty and pre-dictability, social life becomes impossible. There has to be some degree of non-rationality, in the sense of a not completely reasoned and logically watertight adoption of some things as known: a commitment, a decision, a belief in some facts and values, which enables social action to take place.

As noted above, assimilation of some knowledge and a sense of knowing our identity are integral to the educational process. These may be seen as a surrender to some form of rationalist epistemology that, at root, is an emotional embrace of the validity of certain assertions and claims to truth. As Hume observed, ' … belief is more properly an act of the sensitive, than of the cogitative part of our natures' (Hume 1969: 234). The point is, however, that the believing of a claim as true is not the end-point. It needs to be accompanied, as Hume emphasises, by scepticism – a continual asking of critical questions – which acts as a vital guard against dangerous 'flights of the imagination' (p. 314): the very point also of the congregation at the origins of modern Western democracy, in which interpretations were tested and approved as a check on individualist absurdities. The point for educa-tion too is that it is a *process*. Education is not confined to one form of knowledge. There are times for transmission which places emphasis on assimilating knowledge. And there are times when this should be ques-tioned and investigated.

On the basis of the above argument, we have a nice, neat process that will educate young people so that they can take part as autonomous members of democratic society: assimilation (*à la* rationalist epistemology) → questioning and testing (*à la* critical epistemology) → new assimilation, and so on, onwards and upwards. Well, it is not quite so simple. There is a paradox in liberal education. An external influence (school education) is being applied to young people so that they can attain the point where they are not controlled by external influences (Moos 2004). Or, putting it another way, a difficult question is raised by this apparently neat process. How can a way of learning built on acceptance and surrender (assimilation) sustain genuine critical independence? In response, an appeal can be made to five points concerning human capacities and the processes of learning and social action that form an interrelating platform for development of critical independence. The first two basic human capacities are highlighted by Moos, who derives them from traditions in educational thought.

Firstly, people are endowed with 'an innate ability to be open-minded' (Moos 2004: 7). To this I would add that the recognition, valuing and nur-turing of this is an historically situated phenomenon. Secondly, the self has the capability to reflect on both itself and something beyond itself, which 'enables the human being to act and to reflect on the action and thereafter initiate other actions' (ibid.). Thirdly, people have resources within their own selves – the capacity for navigational feelings – that further aid independent scrutiny of external influences.

The fourth point is that reconciliation of such profoundly challenging paradoxes and contradictions is not achieved at the level of ideas, but is reached through practice. What is to be valued and what are to be the norms governing behaviour and how values and norms relate to each other cannot be finally decided upon through discussion and reasoning. As Joas (2000) explains, drawing on pragmatist philosophy in particular, ethical action is always experimental. We can only develop our understanding of what is good and right through creative action which takes place in contingent conditions.

This does not mean that values and norms are arbitrary. It is a recognition that no amount of theorising or deliberation removed from practice can resolve the conflicts and tensions, in particular (concerning democratic leadership for example) those between the democratic principles of freedom, equality, organic belonging and substantive liberty. These have to be weighed up and reconciled as part and parcel of everyday action and decision making, a process which is an integral feature of leadership. Values are not so much 'applied' as continually explored through 'creative and risky performances in action' (p. 170); and because none of us can know for certain what will result from actions, despite our good intentions, our understanding of 'the good and the right will come under pressure of revision' in the light of the actual consequences of actions (p. 171). We can aim to strike the appropriate balance between the democratic goods (such as the democratic principles) and norms (such as fairness and honesty), but at any point in time and practice the question of whether this is the right balance is always open to the test of its actual results. The best that can be claimed is that it is highly plausible that such-and-such a course of action was ethically the best.

So, the difficulties and contradictions within our conjectural maps cannot necessarily be reconciled at the level of ideas. Values and norms, as well as concepts and theories concerning the natural world in its widest sense, are weighed against each other and their appropriateness judged in creative social action. When to assimilate and when to criticise, or encourage criticism, are similarly judgements ultimately made at the level of practice as an art, not as a neat, systematised, prescribed technique.

Fifthly, advancing understanding is not something that is done predominantly alone. Learning is collaborative, not just an individual exercise. Students appear to learn more where they rely not only on themselves, or even their close friendship groups, but mix and draw from others in the class 'as resources for particular skills and episodes of learning' (MacBeath

2004: 44). The point applies to teachers as well. Learning in a democratic way aids the development of independent thinking and creativity, which in turn is fundamental to democracy.

Where does all this discussion of knowledge take us? In summary, what underpins democratic education and the educational role of democratic leadership is an *open approach to knowledge*. By this is meant that understanding and knowledge develop through a continual dialectical movement between a rationalist epistemology (which views certain truths as known and posits fixed parameters of knowledge) and a critical epistemology (which considers that nothing can be taken as true and that all conceptions – all facts, theories, values, social codes and norms – are perpetually open to critique). Integral to advancement of understanding in the open approach is dialogue and the sharing of views, expertise and information amongst networks of learners, and the creative application of tentative knowledges in practical action.

Having completed, with this discussion of epistemology, the conceptual exploration of the developmental conception of democratic leadership, I now turn to consider the link between democratic leadership and learning and pedagogy.

Notes

1   Conjectural maps encompass concepts, ideas and their interrelationships, as well as the affective dimension within which these are set – that is, the feelings and moral approbation that are bound up with the conceptual and theoretical picture portrayed by the map.

6 *Links to learning*

The root of interest in democratic leadership, whether at the level of school governance, school leadership or pedagogical leadership, is its connection with learning. Discussion in this chapter cascades down the traditional hierarchy of schools. After considering the influence of senior leadership, attention is given to the notion of teacher leadership, which is closer to pedagogical practice and is a form of distributed leadership in school education seen by some as having contemporary significance. The chapter then turns directly to the teaching and learning which educational leadership – however it is conceptualised and practised – is ultimately intended to influence. If there is an educational responsibility to promote democratic culture, with epistemological implications, there is a responsibility to examine what this means for educational practice in classrooms and other settings for teaching and learning. It implies pedagogical approaches that are 'participatory, open-ended and interactive' (Clough and Holden 2002: 5). It implies that democratic leadership in schools is concerned with promoting and creating the conditions for democratic pedagogies.

Senior leadership

The effects of democratic governance structures are very difficult to assess and research, as there are numerous intervening factors and variables. Reviewing US research, Croninger and Malen (2002) suggest that there is some evidence of modest, if uneven, improvements in student achievement associated with more decentralised and democratic governance of schools. Improvements seemed to be associated with a mix of factors, including an active school council and school principals who, 'working together, have adopted school improvement plans that promote professional development and focus on strengthening relationships within and beyond the school' (p. 296).

Some research suggests that school improvement and effectiveness are associated with democratic and participatory styles of school leadership (Harris and Chapman 2002; Hallinger and Heck 1999). The evidence is, however, not conclusive. This is in part due to the nature of leadership. In so far as it is conceived as the positional leadership of senior authority figures, leadership is one-step removed from the sharp end of education and is found to have a relatively small, direct, measurable impact on learning. Leadership by principals has, for example, a modest effect on student engagement (Leithwood and Jantzi 2000: 61). On the whole, research studies indicate that senior leadership has some impact on school effectiveness, though it tends to be indirect. They show that impact on learning outcomes is 'largely mediated through the work of staff and the school culture or climate that is created' (Earley and Evans 2004: 335), and such studies 'do not support the image of the heroic school leader' (Hallinger and Heck 1999: 185).[1] These studies comprise part of the ideas context which has galvanised critiques of transformational leadership.

Nevertheless, leadership generally, and democratic leadership in particular, have consequences – explored in this chapter – that are both significant and difficult (though not impossible) to measure. The impact of the leadership of senior authority figures is diffuse and complex. In Chapter 10, instead of a simple conception of leadership agency, the idea of orchestration (Wallace 2003) as a more appropriate description of the leadership of change is highlighted. Senior leaders utilise and fashion a whole range of influencing factors, which include relationships, school structures, resource allocation, symbolic acts and their own behaviour and discourse, to set in motion and sustain school change. This is not a process of linear cause and effect. Nevertheless, how this is done, and to what ends, affects the kind of culture, atmosphere and, ultimately, teaching and learning experiences which characterise the school. Lingard et al. (2003), on the basis of their research, lay stress on senior leadership being modelled on effective classroom practice and creating the conditions for teachers to exercise leadership. In other words, the open approach to knowledge applies to students, teachers and senior school leaders. According to their findings, this means that senior leaders should:

- ensure there are opportunities for staff to comment on and criticise senior leadership (pp. 42–3);

- listen to and engage positively with these comments and criticisms (p. 43);

- encourage and provide opportunities for teachers to engage in shared, critical reflection on their own practice (p. 42);

- recognise and value teachers' professional expertise and judgement (p. 43);

- encourage teachers to take responsibility, initiate change and take risks (dispersal of leadership) (pp. 42, 47, 48);

- be attentive to the emotional well-being of teachers and students (pp. 45, 48);

- reject a deficit model of education which blames students and parents (p. 47);

- create a culture of collective responsibility, which means supporting and caring for each other, particularly in difficult times or when things go wrong (p. 48).

In one of the schools studied, where there was a strong school commitment to certain curricular and pedagogical features which had to be adhered to (such as co-operative learning and the cross-curricular integration of environmental education), a teacher describes what it means to be supported and to have a say. She highlights the importance of freedom which allows her some degree of control (the personal choice dimension of decisional rationality), the consequent scope to be creative, the beneficial impact on her emotionally (therapeutic rationality) and the link with classroom teaching:

> To come into a school where the principal appreciates you as a teacher and says, 'I may not agree with the way you do stuff, but I can see that what you're doing is fine', you feel affirmed by that and the fact that you are supported. It makes such a difference. It is like the kids, I guess. They are getting patted on the head, they're happy, and keep going. We are like them, too. The more we try stuff, the more we learn and soon find out what doesn't work. You are in an environment where you are encouraged to step out of your comfort zone and give it a go. (Teacher, quoted in Lingard et al. 2003: 46)

Another example of the significance of senior school leadership is the democratic school which Trafford has sought to create over many years through his consistent leadership as headteacher. He emphasises the way in which the total environment of the school, suffused by a democratic ethos, positively influences the motivation, confidence and self-esteem of students, and how the ethos reminds everyone that the school is there for the students. As a result, Trafford (2003: 22) is convinced that students achieve more than they otherwise would and concludes that senior leaders can influence learning by creating school environments which:

- treat their pupils with dignity and respect as thinking beings;

- help children to develop the skills of democratic citizenship;

- see giving young people a voice as a means both of protecting themselves and of helping their teachers to find the methods and techniques which will enable them to learn in the best way;

- see pupils as potentially more effective students if they are empowered, trusted and allowed to feel safe and able to express themselves freely and responsibly.

Teacher leadership

If leadership is understood as distributed, it is not confined to the senior leadership, but extends into the process of teaching and learning. Hence, a further dimension of the influence of leadership is its reconceptualisation as distributed and the recognition of the active role of teachers as initiative-takers and influential agents of change. One of the ways distributed leadership is translated into education is through the notion of teacher leadership, though the concept is beset in the literature by overlapping and competing definitions (Muijs and Harris 2003). A delineation of its main dimensions is given by Day and Harris (2003) and summarised in Muijs and Harris (2003). Teacher leaders:

- are mediators of school improvement, who translate its principles into classroom practice and draw on expertise, resources and external assistance to do this;

- help create participative leadership in which all teachers feel part of change and development and have a sense of ownership;

- forge closer relationships with colleagues, through which mutual learning takes place.

The school improvement literature suggests that where there is social bridging within schools, which means 'teachers working democratically, horizontally, to share practice, observe and learn from one another – there is a much greater chance of teacher-led school improvement' (MacBeath 2004: 45). Lingard et al. (2003: 34) found teacher leadership to be associated with pedagogies that enhance students' academic and social progress. Findings from the Australian Leadership for Organisational Learning and Student Outcomes (LOLSO) research project indicate that the most effective leadership for organisational learning and improved student outcomes is 'a principal skilled in transformational leadership and administrators and teachers who are actively involved in the core work of the school (shared or distributive leadership)' (Mulford 2003: 115). There are echoes here of ethically transforming leadership, which combines the essentials of transformational leadership with dispersed empowerment. Mulford continues:

What is especially important is that staff are actively and collectively participating in the school and feel that their contributions are valued – that they are involved in a democracy if you like. (op. cit.: 115)

Key arguments for teacher leadership are that it creates collegial relationships which contribute to school improvement, recognises that teachers' ability to lead significantly enhances quality of teaching, and makes leadership a collective, not an individualistic, endeavour (Muijs and Harris 2003).

But is this the same as democratic leadership, and being part of a democracy, as Mulford suggests? It is possible to see in teacher leadership, or how it is utilised, something of the instrumentalism that underpins much of distributed leadership in practice. It is justified by better results – as another technique in the armoury of school effectiveness and improvement.

[T]he concept of teacher leadership is powerful because it is premised upon the creation of the collegial norms in schools that evidence has shown contribute directly to school effectiveness, improvement and development. (Muijs and Harris 2003: 444)

Teacher leadership, it is claimed, encourages heightened emotional engagement and self-esteem (Muijs and Harris 2003), exactly the sort of effects that help create the sense of vocation otherwise rendered fragile in a social order dominated by instrumental rationality. In other words, teacher leadership can very easily become part of a subtle instrumentalism aimed at manufacturing a re-enchantment of the school order. Certainly it does not mean that school hierarchy is eliminated. Moreover, invisible power[2] still acts as an often quiet and unnoticed filter of creative agency and influence. As Quicke observes, 'reforms which aim to foster collaborative cultures often conceal the extent to which this form of power remains dominant' (2000: 299). Allowing teachers space to have their own vision and mission is too challenging for the regulated education system we have today, Gunter (2001: 127) argues. To this can be added the point that, as noted in Chapter 4, the apparent loosening of traditional bureaucratic and hierarchical constraints does not automatically equate with greater freedom. There are strong trends that create organisational contexts which simultaneously seek to

- free staff to make choices and exercise initiative;

- place them in institutional and cultural frameworks that ensure their values, visions and goals are in alignment with those of the organisation.

Nevertheless, at the same time, there are potentialities for change beyond a more subtle instrumentalism. At its 'most profound', Muijs and Harris argue, teacher leadership offers the potential of 'a "new professionalism" based upon mutual trust, recognition, empowerment and support' (2003: 445). In the interstices of regulatory and organisational frameworks there is scope for creative mediation (Jeffrey 2003); in other words, adapting and reworking at school and classroom level prescriptive regulations and requirements which would otherwise serve to narrow the educational experience of students. Moreover, dispersal of leadership that embraces teachers can encompass aims that promote democracy and social justice. There is some support for this potential in Little's (2003) work, which suggests a growing connection between teacher leadership and broader issues of social justice. For Lingard et al. (2003), the characteristics of teacher leadership found in their study include:

- 'a commitment to making a difference to all students' learning', not just those in the teacher's own classroom or school (p. 37);

- disavowal of a deficit model of education, and instead a search for ways of 'reaching' their students which 'involved considerations of pedagogy and what they as individual teachers could do for their students' (p. 36).

With regard to the concern here with democratic leadership, it is clear that teacher leadership is not *inherently* democratic. But it may be fashioned to be so, thus contributing to a culture that values democratic leadership, principles and ways of working. Teacher leadership can be more than collaboration – 'a narrowly functional activity circumscribed by instrumental rationality', in which colleague teachers are seen as useful sources of information and resources only for the task in hand – and can become collegial: 'a joint undertaking informed by the ideals and aspirations of a collective practice infused by value rationality and the commitment to valued social ends' (Fielding 1999: 17). It is eminently capable of displaying democratic rationalities and aspiring to democratic principles. What is necessary, in the first instance, is to make explicit these aims and ideals. Teacher leadership which aspires to be democratic cannot be solely about having and conveying a vision and mission in the classroom, but must be committed to making into a reality dispersed leadership which creates and nurtures a democratic learning environment.

Democratic pedagogies

Results from a number of sources tend to support the view that 'students in schools know a good deal about learning, about the conditions that encourage it and the conditions that inhibit it' (Flecknoe 2004: 412). Ruddock and Flutter's research with students, for example, suggests that democratic styles of teaching enhance student engagement, interest and motivation. One of their conclusions is that it is often beneficial to consult students about who it is they best work with, rather than 'impose seating patterns that they may find arbitrary and unproductive' (Ruddock and Flutter 2004: 94).

A note of caution, however, should be sounded. More democratic styles of teaching in the classroom are not necessarily effective in the ways expected. In an interesting controlled experiment, Airey et al. (2004) found, contrary to their expectations, that when they specifically investigated the relationship between student attainment, teacher behaviour and student perception of control, there was no significant association between a democratic style of classroom and student academic progress. Even so, their findings showed that with democratic teaching:

- students generally felt better and more positive and had a greater sense of self-control (teachers enjoyed the environment created too);

- whilst there was no common experiencing of more attainment, students who were *successfully* encouraged to take control of their own learning did achieve more.

Attempts to research the precise effects of democratic styles of teaching remind us of the importance of thinking very carefully about the conceptualisation of democratic teaching. For the purposes of the study by Airey et al., democratic teaching was understood as comprising an approach which valued: explanation to students; assessment of pupil work by a parent/carer, teacher and a fellow pupil; plenary sessions where students could present and comment on work; a homework planner and one homework assignment in which the student taught part of a module to a parent/carer. These were the practical features which distinguished it from the established, traditional-style school department's pedagogical model, which essentially comprised 'a diagnostic-informed deficit model, in which the teacher instructs, and provides learning experiences for, the pupils in what they are perceived not to know' (2004: 10).

A democratic model of teaching, however, encompasses more than specific techniques. Glickman describes democratic pedagogy as a pedagogy that

> aims for freedom of expression, pursuit of truth in the marketplace of ideas, individual and group choices, student activity, participation, associative learning, application, demonstration, and contribution of learning to immediate and larger communities. Such pedagogical effort is undertaken in the context of equality for all, consideration of individual liberty and group freedom, and respect for the authority and responsibility of the teacher to set conditions for developmental learning. (2003: 281)

There is much threaded in Glickman's definition. But is it sufficient? To obtain a surer idea of democratic pedagogy, it really needs to be approached from the direction of the essential components of democracy. These comprise the principles and rationalities of developmental democracy (Chapter 2) and the open approach to knowledge (Chapter 5). Having in mind a framing like this, as represented in Figure 6.1, does three things. Firstly, it reminds educational leaders of the scale and ambition of democratic pedagogy. Secondly, it opens up possibilities by asking fundamental questions concerning teaching and learning and the educational relationships within and beyond the school. Thirdly, it helps draw attention to the tensions and dilemmas that inevitably arise in practice, such as that – long recognised – between freedom and equality.

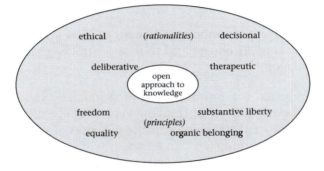

Figure 6.1: Framing of democratic pedagogy

Intersecting with this are the three models of social justice, which impact upon and overlap with the practice of democracy (see Figure 6.2). The discussion below is framed by the components of democratic pedagogy: the democratic rationalities, through which the principles are threaded, and an open approach to knowledge. These do not provide a simple checklist which require ticking as 'all present and correct' in order to constitute democratic pedagogy. Rather, they comprise a set of testing dimensions whose presence and interrelationship require exploration and application in each contingent instance of teaching which purports to be democratic.

Glickman (2003: 282) explicitly states that the 'pursuit of truth' is integral to democratic pedagogy. In other words, it inherently entails *ethical rationality*. Such an overt and unambiguous commitment is unusual in discussion of open and participatory teaching processes. Yet grappling with issues and knowledges in order to understand better ourselves, our environment and our actions is part of education. Such pedagogical practice is an expression of ethical rationality: supporting and enabling aspirations to truth, and the widest engagement of people in this collective quest.

A sophisticated conception of truth is implicit in the sort of perspective that Ruddock and Flutter (2004) advocate: learning (both that of teachers and students) involves gaining 'some sense of mastery over what they do know and what they need to know', knowledge of which 'empowers them to begin a search for new knowledge ... ' (Mitchell and Sackney, 2000: 13, quoted in Ruddock and Flutter 2004: 140). Learning includes getting to grips with matters related to values and norms in order to understand better what is good and right amidst the complexities of social living. The curriculum focus is not solely on test scores, but 'on how to facilitate a personal and collaborative search for a meaningful life' (Henderson 1999: 12) and how teachers can 'find ways to engage their students in personal *meaning making* through passionate inquiry projects' (op. cit.: 12–13, original emphasis).

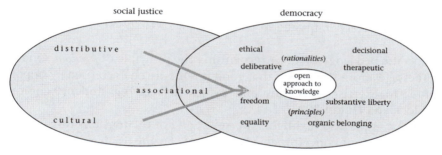

Figure 6.2: Social justice and framing of democratic pedagogy

The connection with *substantive liberty* is clear. Within the perspective of a developmental conception of democracy, pedagogical practice seeks to enable learners to develop their highest potential and to work towards becoming goodly human, as individual and social beings. Their good and the good of others are entwined. The aim of democratic pedagogy is not only to develop skills and knowledge of a range of curriculum areas, but also to encourage people to develop as participating citizens with a sense of the worth and value of transforming social life for the better: 'to lead challenging and fulfilling lives *and* to actively seek the same for others' (Lingard et al. 2003: 22). Development as participating citizens inherently involves encouragement of ethical and spiritual sensitivities which comprise navigational feelings and form part of an integrational approach towards human capacities – seeking recombination and engagement of all creative human capacities through overcoming of internal contradiction. This is so important because at the root of democratic practice is an understanding that we are social and ethical beings, continually engaging in creative social action and influenced by and influencing others.

Decisional rationality in some form is inherent in democratic pedagogy. It involves offering choices, which provides a degree of freedom, but also extending student participation and leadership to negotiating and making decisions about teaching and the curriculum. This is a collective activity. A teacher describes her practice as follows:

> We always negotiate together what we are going to be doing next. So at the end of last year we decided to do Antarctica in the first term. So, during the first term, we sat down and mapped out the rest of the year together. It is 'Just sit on the floor with your piece of paper, and write down where you would like to go for your learning journey.' There were 67 responses. Then we have to sit down together and try and link things and from that we get down to about six. I concentrate on the context, and get the things that I need to teach into it. I don't worry too much about the content. I am more interested in the context behind it. (Teacher, quoted in Lingard et al. 2003: 27–8)

Democratic pedagogy involves recognising the principle of *freedom*. One of the messages from students is that good lessons are characterised by opportunities to exercise autonomy and by teachers giving students choices (Ruddock and Flutter 2004).

This example also highlights, however, one of the tensions involved in practical decisions concerning pedagogy: how far the teacher's authority in the educational hierarchy is relinquished whilst at the same time retaining responsibility and the ability to ensure that learning is advanced. It points to the general issue that tensions between the components of democracy arise when attempts are made to translate them into practice. Not all can be achieved at the same time, and progress in one direction (such as individual freedom) may be at the expense of others (such as unity or equality). Including students in decisional rationality concerning the curriculum could result in decisions that adversely affect educational progress by all or some of the students concerned.

Airey et al.'s (2004) study highlights the differential impact on students of a more democratic teaching style: a minority of students when in a democratically taught module felt less in control and were found to regress in their attainment scores. (Equally, a minority of students in the traditional-style modules were found to regress in their scores because they were deprived of the control which enabled them to learn more.) Moreover, students were by no means always aware of which pedagogical style was the one that led to their individually progressing best (on admittedly narrow academic measures). How effective is freedom and choice if sure knowledge of decisional consequences is lacking?

The point here is not to conclude that hierarchical direction of students is universally the surer pedagogical option. Rather, the point is to recognise that weighing up the appropriate relative emphasis on student rights and their access to decisional rationality on the one hand, and the professional imperative to decide on what is right in given circumstances (with teachers giving a dominant steer in the exercise of ethical rationality) on the other, is subject to the variabilities of local and personal factors. Lingard et al.'s observation is interesting in this regard as it points to the possibilities for continuing subtle control through the exercise of invisible power:

> What is interesting to note [concerning the kind of teaching exemplified by the above quote] is that negotiating the curriculum was not an abrogation of responsibility by teachers. The teacher herself, like many of her students, was a skilled negotiator who was able to ensure that the classroom maintained its intellectual rigour at the same time as allowing student input. (2003: 28)

Power differences are bound to exist. The question is whether the exercise of this kind of influence over the direction of learning constitutes arbitrary power, which by curbing negative freedom (freedom from constraint) is at odds with democratic pedagogy. On the other hand, it might be argued that such subtle directive control is necessary in order to ensure learning that will promote positive freedom (self-mastery) and opportunities to develop substantive liberty. If the latter is the case, ought it nevertheless to be subject to self-conscious legitimation? What is raised here is the question of the limits to associational justice (that is, equal participation and influence in decision making).

A further point to bear in mind is that participation and sharing of leadership provides experiential learning in democratic citizenship. The lessons that come from practical student leadership and democratic involvement, however, are not necessarily straightforward. Asked at the end of a lecture on 'Children as miniature citizens?', what was the point of democratic schooling if the students voted that they found the national curriculum (statutorily required in England and Wales) boring and wanted a different curriculum, the lecturer, Martin Ashley, gave the following answer:

> Children have to learn the limits to democracy and to formulate realistic expectations in relation to their own relationships with their workplace, community and country. One of the most important lessons they have to learn is that they can't always have what they want, but that they have the right to make their wants known and the right to question authority. They need to learn that there are appropriate ways of questioning authority. They need to learn how to use these, how to formulate and present good arguments, and that when

the appropriate channels are pursued, peaceful change is achieved if the arguments are good enough. (Response given by Ashley, in Ashley and Barnes 1999: 149)

This argument illustrates much of the learning about citizenship inherent in democratic practice concerning the practicalities of decisional rationality, the limits of freedom and the importance of skills in exercising discursive rationality. Student democratic leadership is a powerful component of democratic pedagogy. Whilst it can teach students about their relative powerlessness (Lockyer 2003), it can also provide experience of making a difference, contributing to a sense of the world's transformability. Learning environments include student parliaments, such as one cited as being responsible for bringing first-aid teaching to the school, contributing to the local borough's anti-racist policy and establishing a nursery garden to provide trees for the borough's schools (Ashley with Barnes 1999: 148), and which, from this account, appears to have had decisional effects. Exercising practical democratic leadership helps to develop skills necessary for citizenship in a democratic society. These include 'the competence to participate in democratic communities, the ability to think critically and act deliberately in a pluralist world, the empathy that permits us to hear and thus accommodate others' (Barber 1992: 128, quoted in Annette 2003: 143).

Inherent in this sort of participatory citizenship (part of the school's broad curriculum and pedagogy) is *discursive rationality*, which is also manifest in the classroom through dialogue around the curriculum. Dialogue, which may or may not entail decisions and thus involve decisional rationality, is a marked feature of pedagogical discussion associated with learning. There is evidence that 'learning takes place best when a mutually shared understanding between teachers and pupils is built through negotiative discussion' (Jeffrey 2003: 490; see also Woods 1995). An association between the most productive pedagogies and negotiation was found by Lingard et al. (2003: 27). The potential of commentary and feedback from students to improve the organisation and practice of teaching and learning is also evident from a number of studies – in relation to, for example, areas of concern such as transfer to secondary school, how to engage students when engagement sags in Years 3 (age 7/8) and 8 (age 12/13), student self-image as learners, and the qualities of good teachers and good teaching (see Ruddock and Flutter 2004: Chapter 3). One of the strongest themes from students is that how they are treated is as important as how they are taught (ibid.).

Discursive rationality permeates the processes involved in recognising both difference and a shared identity and purpose – in other words, the unity in diversity of *organic belonging*. One example of this is a school where students undertake research on matters such as pedagogic practice, supported and facilitated by teachers, and where there is active student–teacher dialogue (discursive rationality) based on student research findings in a variety of settings which include staff forums and governing body meetings. Fielding, reporting his investigations of the school, highlights the vibrancy of this joint work

> rooted as much in delight in difference [between student and staff perspectives] as in delight in what is shared. That delight and … transformative energy is itself an articulation of the living reality of inclusive community. The dialogic encounters now transforming the structures as well as the culture of that school are an instantiation of the centrality and richness of difference, which is, in turn, transformed into a complex, more demanding unity. (1999: 24)

Crucial to this is a sense of belonging which complements the respect for difference associated with cultural justice. With regard to the broad curriculum, peer group discussion can offer a way of promoting cultural justice. A study by Peck et al. (2002) concerning disabled and non-disabled students found that such discussion, conducted according to democratic principles, effectively promoted inclusion:

> In these meetings nondisabled students freely expressed their experiences, beliefs, and feelings about inclusion and exclusion in their school and classroom. Over time, participating students developed not only a sense of advocacy for their disabled peers, but also a greater sense of belonging for themselves. (Furman 2002: 282)

Democratic pedagogy displays *therapeutic rationality*, empowering and raising the self-esteem of students. It involves aiming to eliminate all of the 'unnecessary pain' which is 'avoidable [yet] become[s] part of classroom practice' – humiliation, blaming and shaming, boredom, imposed silence, loneliness, lack of belonging (Knight 2001: 258). The fundamental starting point is an environment in which children feel 'unthreatened, safe and valued' (Trafford 2003: 20). This positive 'feel' is part and parcel of the ethos that democratic leadership creates and sustains. Therapeutic rationality is also about empowerment through participation. Jeffrey, for example, found that sharing pedagogic understanding and involving students empowered them to take part in evaluations of teaching and learning practices: 'learners had developed a language to conceptualise learning and pedagogy, due to their involvement by teachers in the purposes of lessons and the development of a team culture' (2003: 501).

Democratic pedagogy promotes *equality*, meaning that classroom practices 'are premised on the belief that all students can learn and hence all students regardless of their perceived "ability" ought to be provided with pedagogies and assessment practices that enable them to do so' (Lingard et al. 2003: 20). Equality in this sense does not equate with a rigid uniformity of treatment, but recognises and responds to the diverse needs and cultures of students. The study by Airey et al. (2004) affirms the importance of attending to the potential differential impact of democratic approaches. What equality does mean is 'equal encouragement' (Knight 2001: 261). Knight has in mind that, integral to democratic education, are a number of encouragements to students. These include encouragement to risk (expressing opinions and challenging authority), elimination of avoidable pain (as mentioned above), creating a learning environment that gives everyone a belief in their own competence, a sense of belonging to an inclusive community and a feeling of enthusiasm and ownership in relation to their learning by having space to participate in decisions and discover for themselves.

The point here is that these supports and affirmations of worth need to be operative for all. Rather than a static concept of 'ability', fixed for each student, a more egalitarian approach puts into practice a commitment to the transformability of learning capacity (Hart et al. 2004). Again, the latter commitment reinforces the developmental nature of democracy. Transformability entails some sense of substantive liberty: that there is an inherent human capacity to learn that takes the person towards ways of living and being that are intrinsically worthwhile. That internal capacity can be helped or hindered by external conditions, which include the educational environment for learning.

At a practical level, democratic pedagogy needs to be fashioned in such a way that recognises and addresses the different aspects of inequality. Three are highlighted here. Firstly, there are distributive injustices which obtrude into the processes of learning. Practical issues arise such as differential access to material and informational resources by students and their families. Secondly, there are cultural injustices that characterise society and cross into the school, such as cultural, class, gender and ethnic inequalities and histories of injustice. The desire to address these may lead to an interest in 'disruptive pedagogies' – 'teaching practices which disrupt marginalising processes by encouraging students to identify and to challenge the assumptions inherent in, and the effects created by, discourses constructing categories of dominance and subservice within contemporary society' (Mills 1997: 39).

Thirdly, there is the hierarchy of authority and status within the school-as-community. The implications of considering this and how it may be diminished, if not eliminated, can be discomforting and may begin to challenge existing differences and hierarchies, which reflects the oppositional character of democratic leadership. The teacher is *an* authority, not *the* authority (Kelly 1995).

At the heart of democratic pedagogy is an *open approach to knowledge*. In summary, this involves

- dialectical movement between assimilation and critique, with the latter involving application of critical abilities, drawing off theories of constructivist learning 'which encourage students to construct new knowledge through the use of complex reasoning skills, such as hypothesizing, synthesizing and evaluating' (Lingard et al. 2003: 22);

- creative application in practical action;

- dialogue and sharing of views, expertise and information amongst networks of learners.

This resonates with notions of 'authentic pedagogy', which consists of 'students actively constructing knowledge, using disciplined inquiry and finding applications beyond schools for what they have learned' (Glickman 1998: 32). Research evidence suggests that modes of learning which reflect an open approach to knowledge are valued by students. Ruddock and Flutter emphasise that from their investigations

> again and again in interviews we hear *students'* pleas for more 'autonomy' – by which they seem to mean ... tasks where they can 'work things out for themselves' or learn from each other, and ... learning that they have actively constructed rather than just copied into a notebook. (2004: 83; original emphasis)

Six conclusions concerning links to learning

Six conclusions are suggested on the basis of the foregoing discussion. Firstly, creating a school environment that encourages and values student participation and feedback, and is sensitive and responsive to it, is likely to enhance learning. Lack of sensitivity is more likely to lead to schools and teaching which 'structure and sustain poor self-image in school' (Ruddock and Flutter 2004: 54). Dispersal of leadership to involve students in this sense has a positive relevance for learning and achievement.

Secondly, care is needed not to make unsustainable claims about the benefits of democratic leadership and styles of schooling in terms of measurable academic results. Looking at research evidence reinforces the caution that is required in asserting the benefits of democratic leadership and pedagogy on academic progress. This is not surprising as, at the level of the classroom and the broad school curriculum, there are complex interacting principles and practices to take into account, and hence there is no simple connection with learning.

Thirdly, following from this, democratic pedagogy is a constellation of the principles and rationalities of developmental democracy and the open approach to knowledge. These conceptual components of democratic pedagogy and leadership have to be worked with, recomposed and forged together with different emphases and compromises according to circumstances and contingent possibilities.

Fourthly, the conception of what constitutes valued learning is challenged by democratic leadership founded in a developmental understanding of democracy. If students, and staff, are to be cared for as people, rather than fodder for the economy, a fundamental concern is the experience of education. What does it, and how do we want it, to *feel* like for students, for staff, and for families and communities? Democratic leadership creates a particular texture of relationships which is supportive of all of these members of the school community as creative agents with inherent potential. Moreover, the human development that is integral to this texture of relationships – a sense of mutual identity and support, feelings of empowerment, social and interpersonal capabilities – is itself learning, even if it is not as amenable to measurement as other areas of learning.

Fifthly, internal alignment of leadership approaches within a school is critical. Democratic pedagogy and practice envelop both students and staff in a school if it is to be a community seriously committed to a breadth of meaningful learning. The dispersed professional leadership of senior authority figures and teachers involves the attempt to put into practice the same constellation of the principles and rationalities of developmental democracy characteristic of democratic pedagogy.

Sixthly, in the quest to enhance learning opportunities, the task for senior school leadership is to fashion and encourage the conditions which promote this internal alignment and an open and democratic approach to knowledge and learning.

Notes

1 See also Mulford and Silins (2003) and Witziers et al. (2003).
2 See Chapter 7 on ineffective democracy.

7   *Obstacles and challenges*

This chapter is intended to sharpen the focus on challenges inherent in democratic leadership and obstacles to its realisation, summarised in Figure 7.1. These challenges concern every one who is involved in the circulation of initiative and who, therefore, has some part to play in being aware of and working through them, whether they are involved in democracy-creating, democracy-doing or both. Ideas and practices that help address these are discussed in the course of the chapters which follow on structure (Chapter 8), people (Chapter 9) and practical engagement (Chapter 10).

Context
- non-democratic structure, culture and history of schooling
- adverse political, social and economic forces
- appropriation of 'democracy' and 'democratic leadership'
  - devaluation of meaning
  - colonisation

People
- resistance
  - self-interest
  - traditional deference
  - belief in superiority of hierarchy
  - apathy
  - reasoned scepticism
- capacity problems

Practice
- ineffective democracy
- inauthentic democracy
- misbalances
- minimalism (reduction to competition of interests)
- resources (especially time)

Figure 7.1: Obstacles and challenges to democratic leadership

Context

The context provided by schools is not especially conducive to democracy and democratic leadership. Fielding identifies two sets of difficulties. The first is associated with the 'largely anachronistic structures and cultures' (2004: 309) of schooling which divide teachers and students into two separate and unequal arenas and which represent a structural obstruction to dialogue. It is widely acknowledged that in the UK for example:

> what state and most private schools ... have traditionally taught best is obedience and social conformity. Young people have largely been prepared for an adult life in which they take their place in the hierarchical organizations and associations of civil society. (Lockyer 2003: 127)

The second set is associated with performativity and surveillance which are manifest through school inspections, performance management, publication and tracking of test and examination results, and so on. This 'context of performativity and a narrowly conceived, incessant accountability leads too readily down the path of a carping, antagonistic relationship between students and teachers ... ' (p. 308). The labelling of schools as failures, which is often part and parcel of this context, also has an emotional impact on teachers and others, leading to stigmatisation and lowering of morale (Hargreaves 2004; Woods and Levačić 2002). Ruddock and Flutter note that, 'Teaching for intellectual growth and teaching for examination passes are not necessarily the same and it is not easy in the present climate for teachers to avoid some degree of sacrifice of the one to the other' (2004: 85). A deeper concern is that participation and democracy will be part of what Hartley (2003: 17) calls 'the instrumentalisation of the expressive' and will become, as a result, an aspect of subtle instrumentalism. Democratic leadership has to be qualitatively different from being a means of engendering compliance with dominant goals and values and harnessing staff commitment, ideas, expertise and experience to their realisation.

The depth of the problem is emphasised by the differential impact of a curriculum which is strongly framed and which tends to be underpinned by a rationalist epistemology. Arnot and Reay's (2003) work reveals the problems for student voice and democratic pedagogy in their study of two secondary and two primary feeder schools in very different catchment areas. They make the point that a fixed curriculum which appears irrelevant and disaffecting to many students creates a structural barrier to democratic participation. This is 'likely to be particularly problematic for working class boys who experience daily the strong regulative culture of the classroom and confrontational relations with teachers' (p. 30). They conclude that, if 'strong frames control what can and can't be said, then consulting pupils about their learning is unlikely to make a difference' (p. 30).

Amongst the contextual sources of problems for democratic leadership are political, social and economic contexts inimical to democratic values and practices. The word 'democracy' fully entered the political vocabulary at the end of the eighteenth century, and was often used as a pejorative term. Democrats then 'were seen, commonly, as dangerous and subversive mob agitators' (Williams 1963: 14). The oppositional character of democratic leadership arises from its tension with dominant trends in contemporary educational policy. Democratic rationalities are often uncomfortable bedfellows with the market entrepreneurialism and centralised target-driven demands that form the context for schools. In consequence, democratic leadership involves ideas and actions which challenge market values, instrumental rationality and the evaluation of people's participation according to market and functional criteria.

Material and cultural inequalities that mark the social context of schools also make achievement of democratic leadership considerably more difficult. The more social injustice there is, the harder it is to attain the democratic ideal. The attempt to construct a shared leadership between two principals in a New Zealand school and to build across the school's white middle-class and Maori communities (to develop organic belonging) were eventually defeated by the combined effect of under-resourcing and the subtle ways in which the voices of the less powerful were excluded. Despite the best intentions of the two principals, the 'levels of combined collaborative energy and skill required in day-by-day engagement in such sociocultural, political and economic resource struggles, were ultimately beyond their capabilities' (Court 2003: 180).

Globally, the idea of democracy is assumed to be a taken-for-granted good. But one way of dealing with its essentially oppositional character is to appropriate it and render it harmless. We have seen in Chapter 3 that global trends in economic activities and relationships help to create a perception of demands for certain skills and types of people and a view that school education should be geared to fulfilling these demands. These underlie the interest in distributed leadership. Bottery summarises the promise that some see in all of this:

> [B]ecause of the need for flattened hierarchies, for better trained employees, and for more self-managed task groups, the organization of the future, *it is claimed*, will be more empowering, more organic, more democratic, a more collaborative place to work. (2004: 9; emphasis added)

This is where we can begin to see the potential for appropriation of democracy and democratic leadership. There are two dangers. One is *devaluation of meaning.* In this competitive and stressful climate, there is a danger of democracy and democratic leadership becoming 'aerosol' words (Smyth and Shacklock 1998: 81). This can result in reducing the meaning of these concepts simply to being nicer and more attentive to colleagues. In much influential writing in leadership and management – both generic contributions to the field and specifically educational – democracy and democratic leadership are conceived in ways that divorce them from deeper philosophical and political questions integral to the consideration of models of democracy outlined in Chapter 1. Fullan, for example, defines the democratic leader as one who 'forges consensus through participation', which includes 'seeking and listening to doubters' (2001: 35, 42). Another example is this description of the democratic project leader:

> You *involve* everybody in all aspects of the team's activities. There is more discussion and consultation in decision making and taking. Team member skills and creativity are actively encouraged by you creating a climate to help everybody achieve project, team and personal goals. (Young 1997: 252)

The other, closely related danger – and perhaps of most concern – is *colonisation*, that is of being redefined by ideas and practices which repress the essential vitality and oppositional character of democracy. Instrumental rationality and exchange relationships are powerful forces which are in contention with the developmental conception of democracy and which can lead to progressive, humanist principles and practices of participation being used for disconnected ends of profit-maximisation and achievement of imposed targets. As Blackmore argues in relation to feminist concerns with humanistic participation:

> The dilemma … for feminism is that applying the logic of intimate relations to the political life of organizations is fraught with contradictions (e.g. care and teamwork), as the shared principles of equality, mutuality of respect and consensual decisionmaking in face-to-face contexts idealized in discourses about women's ways of leading cannot be so readily replicated in large organizations or systems, but can still be appropriated by managerialist discourses of consensus, vision and strong culture. (1999: 208)

The democratic company, of which Gratton (2004) writes, has many key elements in common with the ethically diluted conception of transformational leadership influential in education (see Chapter 3). According to Gratton, in companies which resemble the democratic enterprise, the leader's personal philosophy pervades the company (p. 198) and, whilst team leaders expand the space for choice and freedom, at the same time they 'delineate it with the obligations and accountabilities contained with business goals' (p. 198). This kind of leadership – described as democratic – engages and enthuses employees. Its perceived value is what it delivers to the organisation: 'When people are engaged and committed they are more likely to behave in the interests of the company and they have less need to be controlled and measured' (p. 208).

In another example, it is similarly argued that the future of leadership is democratic and that democracy is inevitable 'even in the workplace' (Lawler 2001: 16):

> Hierarchical organizations are simply too inflexible and rigid to compete effectively in today's business environment. They fail to attract the right human capital and to produce the right core competencies and organizational capabilities. As a result, they need to be replaced by lateral forms of organization that rely heavily on teams, information technology, networks, shared leadership, and involved employees ... [These new organizational forms] will have flat, agile structures, open information, power that moves to expertise, and systems that create knowledgeable employees throughout the organization. (Lawler 2001: 16–17)

Democratic leadership, in this view, is a means of engendering compliance with dominant goals and values and harnessing staff commitment, ideas, expertise and experience to realising these. Democracy is instrumental and de-politicised, and has more in common with distributed leadership.

It is possible to see in the concern with student engagement an extension of subtle instrumentalism. Jeffrey (2003: 494) notes amongst teachers a lessening of emphasis on responding to pupils' emotions and on developing pupils' own educational evaluations, and instead 'a more pragmatic use of emotions to engage interest'.[1] A concentration on team identity amongst pupils and teacher encourages learner collaboration and a shared identification with school objectives. In the following example these children, quoted by Jeffrey, are talking about a forthcoming inspection of their school by the national inspection agency in England, Ofsted (Office for Standards in Education), illustrating how subtle instrumentalism can become pervasive:

> 'All the children were really sensible because they wanted to show that our school was the best school. We wanted to get a better report and we were told that if we didn't get a good report we would get into the newspaper.'

'If we had a bad report people might not send their children to the school.'

[About national tests:]
It is hard for the teachers to teach us such a lot and they spend a lot of time doing it. And if we don't get 'level four story' it looks like the teachers have not worked hard enough. If we don't succeed it would have let them down because they have worked so hard trying to get good marks.' (op. cit.: 499)

This kind of development in schools mirrors what is seen to be occurring in organisations generally: the use of distributed leadership and team working to more effectively secure allegiance to organisational values, visions and goals.

People

Distinguishable from these contextual concerns, but not separate from and untouched by them, are the characteristics of the people involved. Moves to democratise leadership can come up against resistance at all levels of an organisation. Influential here are perceived interests and socialisation according to the way things have traditionally been. Having reviewed writings on democracy and democratic leadership, Gastil (1997) concludes that there are four main reasons why leaders reject it as a model of leadership:

- a perception that it threatens their own, non-democratically legitimated authority;

- a belief that strong, directive authority is just and efficient;

- an emotional need for a strong leader – the 'unconscious or conscious desire for a hero, a charismatic figure capable of solving our problems and sweeping away our confusion' (p. 168);

- or, contrary to the previous reason, a lack of faith in leaders of any kind, whether democratic or non-democratic.

The degree to which headteachers and school principals are committed to democratic leadership is a moot point. In the UK, Grace (1995: 202) drew attention to how very small the number of 'committed headteacher-democrats' is and comments how, in the English school tradition, '[h]ierarchy is taken to be an inevitable feature of schools' (Grace 2001: 239). In a study of 81 experienced teachers in the USA, Spaulding found that the overwhelming majority 'reported that new teachers need to know how to identify and respond to the political manoeuverings or strategies of the principal ... It was clear from our research that political behavior permeated life in schools and that teachers saw the role and the person occupying the role of school principal as politically powerful' (1997: 41). Fewer than one in six described 'a present or past principal as democratic with behaviors that resulted in positive consequences for teachers and teaching' (p. 54). Spaulding concludes that ' ... many contemporary school teachers would agree that the autocratic principal is still alive and well, although disguised under a blanket of democratic terminology' (p. 52).

The habits of hierarchy can also be deeply ingrained in teaching staff. This is illustrated by a study by MacDonald of a Scottish primary school:

> Far from adopting the collegiate model which [the headteacher] attempted to foster, [the teachers] perceived their head teacher to be in authority over them in matters relating to the school, leaving little locus for collegiality ... They perceived social distance and deferential behaviour to be fitting to the head teacher/teacher relationship and carefully maintained the existing power relationship. (2004: 431)

Goldstein undertook research into distributed leadership, associating it with a 'countervailing vision for education ... that would flatten the hierarchy and vest teachers with authority and responsibility for the quality of education' (2003: 399). The focus of her research was an initiative to move responsibility for teacher evaluation from school principals to teachers who could engage in peer review and support. She found, however, that after the initial redistribution of authority and control, 'people regressed to that which was familiar' (p. 416), namely the previous hierarchical model of authority. The same conservatism can be found beyond staff also. For example, democratic participation can be forestalled or limited by parental apathy and parents' traditional expectations regarding the headteacher or principal (Blase and Blase 1999).

To these perceptions should be added reasoned scepticism. There are sometimes good reasons to be sceptical of the promises of participation and more democracy. There are real difficulties and costs in their implementation, and, as was highlighted in the previous chapter, it is important to be guarded and cautious in claims as to the benefits in terms of learning. Therefore, in considering democratisation of leadership, proper regard needs to be given to issues of its timing and interconnection with other, parallel changes and pressures, the challenges it poses to participants, and its practical consequences for different people in the particular circumstances and cultural history of an organisation. In summary, resistant attitudes can result from:

- self-interested attachment to existing power relations;

- traditional deference to hierarchy;

- belief in the superior effectiveness of hierarchy;

- apathy;

- reasoned scepticism.

Another difficulty faced in dispersing democratic leadership results from capacity problems. Demands are placed on leaders and potential leaders in terms of their aptitudes, skills and commitment which not all staff or students are equally placed to meet. Different stakeholder groups – professional educators as against others for example – are likely to have differential capacities. Where the concern is to include local communities and parents, for example, they do not necessarily possess equal leadership capacities to involve themselves in governance. Some parents are more able to take the lead than others. There may well be a wide gulf between educational professionals and the local community. Suzuki for example, in a study of primary school governing bodies in Uganda, found

> an evident power imbalance between parents and headteacher that hinders parents from accessing the information they need … Many parents are … concerned about the school but feel intimidated when asking questions to the headteacher or even to the ordinary teachers … (2002: 252).

Practice

A further set of challenges concerns the tensions and problems involved in the practical realisation of democratic leadership and schooling. These practicalities involve not simply technical questions concerning 'rational selection of instrumental alternatives' in a context where goals and values are given, but also practical questions in which the choice or validity of values, norms and goals are open for questioning and determination (Habermas 1974: 3). In considering these, a familiar duality will be a constant presence: the concern to preserve the integrity of democratic leadership and the need to be realistic in given contexts.

The first problem is that efforts to be more democratic may result in *ineffective democracy*; that is those situations where leaders are sincere in seeking a more democratic leadership, but the framework of power relations remains unchanged and subverts good intentions. As Gunter explains, 'The traps could be in trying to bring about democratic educational change in one-to-one encounters, or the classroom, or the staffroom, in a field of power that is able to control and finance undemocratic prescriptions that have an educational gloss' (2001: 137). There are two dimensions to this potential for inequality:

- inequalities *within* each stakeholder group – professional educators, non-professional staff, students, parents/local communities;

- inequalities *between* stakeholder groups.

Inequalities stem from the uneven distribution of various resources. This includes differences in experience and capacity for leadership alluded to, as well as inequalities in access to the financial resources and facilities that help people to involve themselves and make an impact. With ineffective democracy the power differences remain the dominant arbiter of relationships, despite well-meaning attempts to democratise leadership. The question here is partly to do with formal power relations and rights to access material and symbolic resources – *visible power*. But it is also to do with the fact that power is not reflected simply in such formal arrangements. Democratic leadership involves recognising the dispersed nature of power that works quietly and is often unnoticed, that is, *invisible power* which threads itself through relationships, cultural symbols and everyday patterns of social living. The 'continual reinforcement of differential power relationships' results in formal, senior leadership roles in particular

> acquiring a form of social capital that becomes a taken-for-granted reality: a position of privilege and political leverage over others that these others do not question. (Ray et al. 2004: 323)

Consequently, community representatives involved in democratic governance structures very often find themselves dealing with relatively minor or marginal issues, rather than the central educational concerns of the school or college (Croninger and Malen 2002: 297). Experience and research over some time suggest that, in the USA for example, opportunities for 'meaningful parental participation and influence in local [site-based school] councils are rare, especially for parents of children from low-income populations' (ibid.), notwithstanding that evidence of more positive examples of participation is apparent too (Martin 1999).

A specific contributor to ineffective democracy is *unrepresentativeness*. For example – if we stay with the issue of school-community relations – the aim of ensuring that governing bodies are genuinely representative is a perennial problem. The community may in fact be made up of very different communities or groups. Middle-class parents tend to be more involved in school forums for participation than poorer, disadvantaged families (Vincent and Martin 2005). Children's perspectives may differ from their parents and other adults in the community. Those who share membership of a particular social or ethnic group do not necessarily possess views or behaviours in common. Communities and their representatives may be distant from each other. For example, Suzuki's (2002: 252) study found that the 'distance' as perceived by parents between themselves and local leaders on the parent-teacher association and the domination of governance positions by the local elite meant that 'ordinary parents are reluctant to ask questions that challenge their leaders' (p. 252). (See also Deem et al., 1995.)

Families have diverse needs and preferences and varying economic and cultural resources, affected by social class, ethnicity and gender. A study by Rose of community participation in Malawi showed the barriers to involvement by women in the community. The findings are worth quoting at some length.

> In terms of the composition of school committees, attempts have been made to ensure diversity of their membership in particular to include women, with the policy stipulating that one-third of places should be reserved for females. In reality it was evident from discussions held with school committees that women either did not turn up to the meetings or, if present, would often not speak. Furthermore, women continue to be outnumbered on the committees as, in many cases, the quota was not met and was never exceeded. At seven of the 20 schools visited there were no women on the committee, with none of the schools in the North having a female member. At one school, it was noted that the lack of women on the school committee was because, although they had been selected, they refused to join the committee because they said that they have too much work to do in their village. Although attempts at improving gender equity in decision-making at the school level were evident, in practice the involvement of women was at best limited to giving them a place on the committee, rather than ensuring their active participation. (2003: 61)

In contrast to ineffective democracy, *inauthentic democracy* is where the motive to introduce democratic practice is not a genuine commitment to enhance democracy and to effect real democratic leadership, but to give the appearance of more democratic relations. This is about bogus empowerment, driven by ends other than enabling the sharing of leadership and increasing the democratic accountability of leadership. Inauthentic democracy is like Hargreaves' (1994) notion of contrived collegiality, which is 'about creating an illusion of support for pre-determined decisions: at best an advisory service, and often a control device' (Bennett and Anderson 2003: 2). Those trying to introduce inauthentic democracy are helped where they can use as a legitimising device the kind of colonised vision of democracy discussed above.

Apparent moves to enhance democracy may be motivated, for example, by the desire to obtain the benefits of therapeutic rationality – for the advantage of the organisation – without the other dimensions of the developmental conception of democratic leadership. This involves 'the use of therapeutic fictions to make people feel better about themselves, eliminate conflict, and satisfy their desire to belong (niceness); so that they will freely choose to work towards the goals of the organization (control of individualism), and be productive (instrumentalism)' (Ciulla 1998: 68). The problem here is that therapeutic rationality becomes the sole concern, eclipsing especially the challenging ethical and decisional rationalities essential to democratic practice. The 'bottom line' is enhancement of morale and staff satisfaction in the pursuit of organisational effectiveness, with participative decision making being seen as 'a managerial strategy to increase control, not reduce it' (Blackmore 1990: 254) and acting as a device by which to socialise more effectively staff, students and local communities into organisational values and goals. Pseudo-participation takes different forms (see Table 7.1), for example, a managerial approach which manipulates formal structures; an interpersonal technique which places the emphasis on private, informal persuasion; or an adversarial approach which plays out on a public stage to obstruct and undermine differences of view.

Table 7.1: Forms of pseudo-participation (from Ball 1987: Table 5.1, p. 124)

	Forms	Response to opposition	Strategies of control
Managerial	formal committees, meetings and working parties	channel and delay	structuring, planning, control of agendas, time and context
Interpersonal	informal chats and personal consultation and lobbying	fragment and compromise	private performances of persuasion
Adversarial	public meetings and open debate	confront	public performances of persuasion

Ambitions, conflicts and differences of interest are carried into democratic arrangements, and are not automatically or effortlessly resolved by their inception. Participation in practice can work in different, less desirable ways than according to the image portrayed by the ideals of democracy. This is illustrated by a number of diverse examples:

- *containment of participation.* Policies to democratise governance may be met by concerted attempts by professional educators to minimise effective participation by parents and others (Croninger and Malen 2002: 297). Exemplifying the managerial form of pseudo-participation (see

Figure 7.2), there is the 'cleverly autocratic' approach of the headteacher in one study where it was observed how she contrived staff meetings in which critical contributions were allowed but no real opposition tolerated: methods of manipulation included pre-arranging in her office the dialogue that would take place between her and the deputy headteacher in staff meetings (Willmott 2002: 175).

- *deflection of participation.* Participation is in practice shifted into becoming something else. The in-depth study of community participation in 20 schools in Malawi found that the involvement was 'extractive', where members of the local community 'were expected to provide monetary and non-monetary contributions to schools without having any role in deciding how these contributions should be used' (Rose 2003: 57). Moreover, the burden of contributions to community projects in terms of time and money was spread unequally amongst the community. It was more difficult for poor households to contribute and cases were found of families which could not contribute anything and, as a result, withdrew their children from the school, thus exacerbating existing educational inequalities.

- *participation as a means of divesting responsibility for problems.* In South Africa, for example, some see cynical motives behind devolving power to governing bodies, interpreting it as a means by which national authorities transfer to others responsibility for intractable problems (Bush and Heysteck, 2003).

- *thinning of democratic relations.* As observed in Chapter 6, learning is not just an individual exercise: students learn more when they draw from others in the class 'as *resources* for particular skills and episodes of learning' (MacBeath 2004: 44; emphasis added). There is a danger that, wittingly or unwittingly, democratic pedagogies framed in this way may encourage habits of exchange in which people and consequences are judged in instrumental terms. What is created is not so much developmental democracy, more a form of 'consumer democracy' which values collaboration instead of competitive relations, though still focused (in the liberal minimalist mode) on self-interest.

Both ineffective and inauthentic democracy may lead to what Couto calls psycho-symbolic empowerment, which 'raises people's self-esteem or ability to cope with what is basically an unchanged set of circumstances' (Ciulla 1998: 64). What ineffective and inauthentic democracy do not help to achieve is psycho-political empowerment which 'increases people's self-esteem *and* results in a change in the distribution of resources and/or the actions of others' (p 64; emphasis added). Both ineffective and inauthentic democracy may also achieve the opposite of psycho-symbolic empowerment, by lowering morale and self-esteem where participants see the lack of genuine democratic change (intended or not) and feel cheated and at a disadvantage in relationships.

Another of the potential dangers of democratisation is striking *misbalances*, in other words, failing to strike the right balance between all the factors that need to be weighed up in settling democratic arrangements. There is much scope for misjudgement of necessary balances concerning where boundaries of participation should be drawn, what issues different stakeholder groups should deliberate and decide upon and how different interests should be weighed against each other.

> [A]ny democratic settlement of schooling … has to produce an equitable and effective representation of the interests of the central and local state, the interests of the education professional and the students, and the interests of local, democratic community. (Grace 1995: 202)

Grace goes on to observe that a 'major problem in accomplishing such a settlement lies in the sheer difficulty of achieving such a balance, which is, in the last analysis, a balance of power' (p. 202). There are three issues bound up with this, to which I shall return in Chapter 10.

Firstly, there are the boundaries of participation. Where should these be drawn? Who should exercise leadership? Human status may demand inclusion in boundaries of leadership, but there are a number of factors which legitimately should be taken into account in considering the degree to which all possible stakeholders are to be included in democratic processes.

Secondly, there is the degree of participation. How much influence should be exercised democratically by different groups and individuals? Bottery (1992) distinguishes between

* pseudo-participation, in which influence is only apparent;

* partial participation, in which there is limited influence 'conditioned by the greater influence of others' (p. 176);

* full participation, which involves 'equal influence on decisions with all other interested bodies' (p. 176).

Thirdly, there is the scope of participation. What should be open to democratic decision and influence? The scope of dispersed leadership – that is the terrain of issues and organisational activities open to independent initiative – may be circumscribed and differ (sometimes rightly) within and between groups. Should team working be confined to finding creative and effective ways of overcoming specific problems and reaching pre-defined goals?

What issues and decisions ought to be open to school staff, student, parental and community participation?

A further problem is that attempts to create a rich form of democracy may in practice lead to a *minimalist* form. Phillips (2005), for example, draws attention to how democratic participation can be reduced to the competition of interests. Measures that may help counter ineffective democracy include enabling disadvantaged groups to have their own 'space' to develop confidence and leadership capacity and creating quotas for under-represented groups on participatory bodies. But, Phillips suggests, such measures 'could lock people more tightly into an interest group politics where everyone becomes exclusively engaged in battling for their own group's concerns' (p 95). This alerts us to a general danger that a narrow conception of democracy may in practice be enacted, in which the principles of liberal minimalism come to dominate, at the expense of deliberative democracy. The upshot of this is that democratic leadership will tend towards the championing of sectional interests.

Finally, a practical issue is that of finding the *resources* needed to enable dispersed democratic leadership to be active, a major part of the required resource being time (Blase and Blase 1999). As Reitzug and O'Hair acknowledge, time 'needs to be discovered or created for members of school communities to collaborate with each other and to be able to plan and implement frequently labor-intensive democratic practices' (2002: 139). This constraint cannot be underestimated in the practical, day-to-day life of educational institutions. Whether and how it is tackled depend to a great degree on the value placed on democratic principles and practice as essential and defining features of good education.

Having sharpened the focus on challenges and obstacles, in the three chapters which follow attention is turned to what is entailed in creating and sustaining democratic leadership.

Notes

1 This can be read as more psycho-symbolic empowerment (raising subordinates' self-esteem without increasing their power to influence or effect change) than psycho-political empowerment (raising both subordinates' self-esteem *and* their relative power). See the discussion on pp. 84–5.

8 · Free space and firm framing

Reitzug and O'Hair (2002: 139) make two key points about democratic leadership: that it should be neither passive nor hierarchical, but 'proactively democratic', and that a democratic community is an ideal to strive towards – 'not a destination, but rather a journey'. This chapter, with Chapters 9 and 10, addresses what democratic leadership involves in order to make progress on that journey. The ideas discussed in their various ways contribute to tackling the obstacles and challenges set out in the previous chapter.

The chapters are organised around the three-part framework (the trialectic) discussed in the Introduction:

- structural properties: the cumulative consequence of people's agency (this chapter);

- people: capabilities and properties of individuals (Chapter 9);

- practical engagement: individual and collective agency which is enabled by and interprets structural properties (Chapter 10).

Much of the research about democratic and distributed leadership and participation in education shows the positive contribution of a strong framework of values, purposes and structures. Strong central direction is certainly a feature of many instances of distributed leadership (Bennett et al. 2003a; Woods et al. 2004). But it seems counter to the spirit of democracy that all the structural properties of the organisation are firm and set, even if at one time they were determined democratically. In fact, the point is that democracy has a bivalent character (Woods 2004). That is, it requires an organisational dynamic that allows for movement between relatively tight and relatively loose structural frameworks.

On the one hand, people need firm structures – a degree of firm framing. They need a sense of position and place in an organisation, concepts and ideas and a context of values to relate to, and a rhythm of social relationships into which they weave their own activity. They need the structural pathways and signs that are the product of the cumulative organisational footprints of past actions. But these are not rigid, unchangeable facts of social life. If they are approached as such, people's inherent human capacity to move their understanding and practice forward is denied. What we meet again is the importance of a critical approach to knowledge. Social life involves a process of discovery, which leads to advances in understanding and how things are done. Instead of alienation, the aspiration is to 'self-conscious self-determination'.[1]

Hence, also needed, amongst the conditions for discovery, is free space; loose-structured creative social areas where hierarchy and assumptions of knowledge, norms and practice are minimised. These encourage the emergence of new questions, challenging cultural comparisons and connections, and differing, marginalised perspectives. They are similar to what Turner describes as 'anti-structure', which facilitates 'the liberation of human capacities of cognition, volition, creativity, etc. from the normative constraints incumbent on occupying a sequence of social statuses, enacting a multiplicity of social roles' (1982: 44).

So, we can think of the democratic structure of an educational institution as expressing this bivalent character through two forms of structure:

a tight firm framing
which embraces and protects
looser free space.

The sociologist, Georg Simmel (1997: 141), wrote of the metaphor of the picture frame, which is perhaps useful to bear in mind in understanding this bivalent character. The picture frame preserves distance and protects the inner picture. At the same time it presents, strengthens and organises the 'weaker' inner part (the picture itself). In organisations, this 'weaker' part comprises the free space where hierarchy and assumptions of knowledge and practice are minimised relative to the tighter frames of everyday practice. The metaphor of the picture frame can be linked to Basil Bernstein's concept of framing, which concerns how relations and, more particularly, discourse and the creation of meanings are regulated. Bernstein's concept of framing 'refers to relations between transmitters and acquirers' and is 'concerned with *how* meanings are to be put together, and the nature of the social relationships that go with it' (1996: 27). Free space is characterised by weak framing, opening possibilities that are closed in strongly regulated settings. The point about the bivalent structure of democracy is that it entails a relatively strongly framed context which enables free space to exist and foster creative social interaction and learning.

Free space

Let us start with the 'inner picture'. Free space allows interaction and deliberative exchange without the usual constraints of hierarchical and bureaucratic relations or the social and competitive pressures and distinctions that characterise performative and market cultures. Structure is not completely absent, but this space is radically different from the conventional structures that pattern and construct everyday encounters. Highlighted here are two of the forms that free space may take and which can be designed into the structural frame.

The first takes the form of *independent zones*. These are spaces where marginal, disadvantaged and less powerful groups have opportunities to come together and deliberate. They allow a degree of protection from the pressures of dominant interests, ideas and presuppositions. Vincent and Martin (2005) suggest that creating protected spaces for disadvantaged groups is a way of enabling them to contribute to open dialogue. They highlight a number of concepts in the literature that have sought to describe these sorts of spaces: 'counterpublics', 'protected enclaves', 'micro-public spheres'. Who might be the subordinate group differs according to context. It may be parents as a group; it may be a certain section of parents, such as newly arrived refugees and asylum seekers within a particular area (O'Neill et al. 2003); or students as a group, or particular sections of the student population.

The promise of such spaces is that they enable 'deliberative conversation away from the gaze of the dominant group' and development of distinctive agendas and priorities (Vincent and Martin 2005: 126). Research by Vincent and Martin into examples – including a parent education group and a self-help group of African-Caribbean parents – showed that they were fragile institutions, sometimes co-opted by education professionals and limited in their influence on the education system. More optimistically, they also showed a resilience enabling them to survive, and there were positive 'instances of parental voice and engagement in individual schools' (p. 134).

Different types of independent zones for students are possible. They can be built into peer mediation schemes for example. In some schools, student mediators are given space to reflect amongst themselves on their role and take 'time together for self-critique and peer feedback regarding their successes and difficulties in handling particular conflicts … ' (Bickmore 2001: 150). Schools' councils or parliaments have the potential to constitute independent zones, in so far as they provide a protected space for students where they feel able to speak and discuss matters freely.

A different type of independent zone is structured into the life of virtually all schools. This is students' playtime or breaktime. Away from the attention of adults and the structure of the classroom, these provide a time when pupils can find freedom and a social life independent of the classroom, where the rules of conduct are more their own, and where activities stem from their own initiative. (Blatchford 1998: 1).

Independent zones for staff are possible too. Team-working may provide for staff space and time that is removed at least to some degree from senior leadership. Collaborative working and shared leadership amongst groups of teachers are characteristic of much innovative and activist teacher professionalism (Sachs 2003). A school principal in Australia explained how a project team of teachers was given the organisational space and time to develop a common set of ideas about pedagogy. As he described it, they 'sort of wandered around looking for a bigger statement, a clearer vision statement of where they wanted to go' (quoted in Lingard et al. 2003: 120). The result was not a talking shop, but pedagogical change driven by the project group in the light of its explicitly articulated vision. In Blue Mountain School, Canada – extolled as a learning community – teacher teams are an integral part of the organisational structure, meeting monthly to 'determine directions while providing professional learning and development' (Hargreaves 2003: 107).

A second form that free space can take is as *blurred-status arenas*. These are spaces for informal interaction across social and organisational boundaries, bringing together members of social groups or organisational categories differentially positioned in relation to each other in terms of their power, authority and standing. These interactions are uninhibited by the conventions attached to these differences. Blurred-status arenas are areas and times in which organisational members engage with each other without the constraints that characterise usual status distinctions and hierarchical distributions of authority (or at least with a significant reduction of these constraints). One of the forms this can take is the 'carnival' or third place (Sidorkin 1999); a point in time in which the familiar conventions of everyday hierarchy are replaced by free exchange, collective activities and spontaneous dialogue. Sites for these may include cafés, pubs, and other spaces which provide regular retreats and special events. Sidorkin cites an example of a formally planned opportunity for such a space – the traditional Spring *sbor* of a Moscow school:

Up to two hundred children and adults go out of town, or isolate themselves some other way. They have around three very intense days (with very little sleep, which seems to boost creativity) filled with skit-making, fun, far-too-serious discussions, some physical work and sports, and games ... On its surface, the *sbor* is mostly filled with skit-making, quite elaborate in some cases. However, the educators and elder students attach a specific meaning to it, a meaning sharply different from simply having fun. In fact, they perceive it as a work, as a duty, as a demanding service. For an individual, *sbor* is a spiritual experience more than anything else. Being a part of some greater whole, a communion, if you please, is the goal; skits, arts, planning, doing dishes, and even helping the neediest are the means to achieve that goal. (Sidorkin 1999: 138)

Third spaces are for engaging with others and disengaging with the usual and so for Sidorkin they are a 'mechanism that creates the possibility for the genuine dialogue to happen' (p. 136). Integral to these status blurring third spaces is laughter and its potential to subvert the rigidities of ingrained custom and habit. Democracy, like any society, 'needs people not to take it too seriously'. Laughter is integral to understanding: to make sense of things we 'challenge, deconstruct and ridicule' (p. 137). Fielding (2004) observes that there are by and large no shared spaces for teachers and students in which they meet as equal partners, sharing communication and spontaneous dialogue. In other words, third places are generally absent. But perhaps it is also true that we are insufficiently aware of passing encounters and spaces that do exist but remain unacknowledged, in which exchange exists relatively free of conventional status differences (corridor and playground encounters between teachers and students for example). Sidorkin urges alertness to these, as their significance is often missed in research into what are perceived to be good schools.

As well as the carnival-type third places upsetting conventional hierarchy, blurred-status arenas can be more formally enshrined as spaces for specific governance and leadership activities. They can be envisaged as 'little polities' within or related to the organisation. Unlike independent zones, little polities as blurred-status arenas do not separate the non-professional group from professional educators (Vincent and Martin 2005). In addition, they provide for a sharing of power and definite rights to make or contribute to decisions. These arenas thereby become areas for decisional rationality. They may be manifest in two ways.

One is as specific and different spaces within the organisation. Thus school governing bodies, student councils and the like can become spaces for dialogue and decision in which participants engage with each other not solely as hierarchically ordered holders of designated positions and expertise. These blurred-status arenas comprise formal structures in the operational life of the school. Another way is for status blurring to permeate much or all of the organisation. This could involve the sort of whole-school structural change which some advocate in order to create a learning organisation. Such wholesale change involves not only distribution of leadership across a much flatter hierarchy, but also challenges to assumptions about the distribution of knowledgeability and capability – namely, the assumption that the latter are positively associated with formal authority (see Bennett et al. 2003b). Whole-school structural change along these lines makes the whole organisation, at least rhetorically, a blurred-status arena. Trafford (2003) argues, in effect, that much of the democratic school constitutes such an arena. In this context, the practical distinction between the areas of free space and firm framing become less sharp. However, it is difficult to envisage an organisation such as a school dispensing entirely with areas of its institutional, cultural and social life that are relatively firmly framed and fixed.

Incorporating and allowing free space to flourish within a determinate organisational framework is probably the most difficult and challenging for the school as a social order that incorporates and mirrors (to a greater or lesser degree in differing schools and circumstances) societal assumptions of hierarchy and status distinctions. Free spaces may seem to be dangerous, raising fears of uncertainty and chaos. But, as well as being essential to discursive rationality, they can offer new ways of collectively generating insights and values and of offering opportunities for self-transcendence through the alteration to the everyday which they represent. In some ways they may be reminiscent of a spiritual journey: ' ... leaving the certainty, security and apparent wealth of the known, for the uncertainty, insecurity' of the wilderness, a 'place for rethinking, re-orientating, shedding encumbrances and beginning again' (Rees 1987: 51). Integral to the aspiration to democratic leadership is recognition of the importance of embracing creative space as necessary for human creativity and, hence, for liberty.

Free space helps to remove impediments to people becoming participants in the democratic epistemology which the origins of modern democracy made possible, by utilising and developing their own navigational feelings. Hence it is crucial for ethical rationality. In other words, this free, creative space is not significant solely for its consequences for the individual. It is not simply the terrain for an inner, personal exploration. In tandem with formal organisational change that alters the distribution of formal, visible power, free space brings the potential of individual knowledges to bear on organisational affairs and challenges the effect of power on truth. That is, free space provides an arena which challenges the day-to-day reality whereby 'people who hold positions of dominance, by virtue of the acceptance by others of their superiority, become legitimate "carriers of meaning" and "producers of truth"' (Ray et al. 2004: 324).

Firm framing

An environment characterised by dispersed democratic leadership requires not an absence of firm framing but a form of framing that provides a context which tends to generate certain effects, influences and encouragements. The question that needs to be asked is what does firm framing need to address, in order to provide structural support for democracy and democratic leadership in an educational institution? Structural reinforcements and opportunities for democratic rationalities are necessary components of firm framing. This means that:

- institutional provision for decisional rationality is needed, as well as positive affirmation of rights and capacities to participate in decision making;

- the democratic environment should be one which expresses and reinforces a commitment to aspiration to truth – the kernel of ethical rationality – and this needs to be embedded in the influencing ideas and ideals of the democratic school;

- opportunities for deliberative democracy, and reinforcement of the value of discursive rationality are required;

- the whole structure works to affirm self-esteem and convey a sense of being valued to all participants, to encourage therapeutic rationality.

This general answer is now elaborated in relation to the component dimensions of organisational structure: the institutional, cultural and social structures.

Institutional

There is a variety of dimensions to the institutional ways of broadening the leadership base and formally dispersing authority and influence. Not all of these will be appropriate at specific times and for all schools.

Firstly, there are the school's governance arrangements. Opportunities for democratic leadership need to occur in the context of some form of *democratic governance*, in other words, some process and institutional set up that provides a focus for the different parts of the school community, either directly or through representatives, to make or influence key policy decisions, hold post holders to account and to participate in the processes of decision making and discussion. These are polities that facilitate dialogue and debate, and, if they are to disperse democratic leadership, power sharing. Assessing the degree to which these arrangements are democratic involves thinking about the extent to which people – the stakeholders in schools – are given specific entitlements and decisional rights to exercise decisional rationality (voting on decisions, choosing representatives, and so on) and discursive rationality (participating in debates, and being enabled to do this by receiving information, support and the like). Accountability, if it is to mean anything, must have 'teeth': role holders must be made 'liable to review and the application of sanctions if their actions fail to satisfy those with whom they are in a relationship of accountability ... ' (Kogan 1986: 18).

Democratic governance may be institutionalised in the form of one body, with its membership, functions and powers mandated by the state. Thus in this way, for example, school governing bodies in England and Wales and in South Africa are given a key role at school level. These are representative bodies of the *general polity* comprised by the school-as-community and the community in which the school is embedded.

On the other hand, specific polities give opportunities for particular stakeholders. A key example is the scope given to *student polities*, which include student councils and parliaments. Research suggests that the most significant experience of democratic participation is in those councils where students are not only heard and consulted but are given powers and responsibilities and where students are aware that the council 'makes decisions that affect their lives ... can change things in a real way and ... have confidence in its power to do things' (Inman with Burke 2002: 7). The invisible power of professional control is an issue with councils that are set up within the school for students, but not necessarily *by* students. To what extent in their operations do they frame and protect free space that facilitates independence, confidence and creativity? One headteacher in England candidly explained about his school's student council:

> Discussion of the curriculum is not actively discouraged, but I think that the pressures of [national school] inspection and the National Curriculum have reduced student chances to talk about subjects and curriculum balance. It must be admitted that not having another lobbying sector to contend with suits our own very pressured management group. (Cunningham 2000: 138)

In another case, however, researchers illustrated the potential for some measure of independence, despite a degree of control by the headteacher:

> the students retained considerable power over the direction of the meeting. There were numerous occasions where students challenged the Headteacher's interpretations, rejected her suggestions and offered alternative views and strategies ... Whilst we see problems in the control by the Headteacher, none of the students we interviewed shared our concerns, rather they saw the council as 'theirs' and talked positively about the meetings. (Inman with Burke 2002: 43)

Secondly, developing the scope for democratic leadership involves attention to the potential for dispersing leadership through *changes in institutional leadership roles*. One change that may be appropriate in some contexts is co-principalship. Initiatives to share leadership, through co-principalship, can act to loosen internal institutional boundaries in schools and thereby help create better conditions for democratic practice, 'by breaking down hierarchical principal/teacher and professional/lay divides' (Court 2004: 190). This is an example of a structural arrangement (co-principalship) creating and framing (potentially) opportunities for blurred-status arenas to emerge, weakening the status and authority boundaries that mark hierarchical divides.

Another focus for change in institutional leadership roles is the expansion and design of institutional arrangements for networks and groupings specifically to enhance opportunities for dispersal of leadership, taking initiatives and sharing responsibility with others. These include:

* ad hoc, short-term, task-specific groups or committees which draw in expertise and views from throughout the school community;

* longer-term (standing) groups, including 'cross-sectional ... liaison groups' which bring people together from different departments (Blase and Blase 1999: 485).

Amongst these sorts of institutional arrangement are specific programmes, such as peer mediation programmes which build into the structural properties of a school dispersed participation and learning opportunities about active democratic citizenship (Bickmore 2001). Framed within broad values – a safe and peaceful environment for example – competing and conflicting perspectives on what is good and right in specific situations have to be reconciled through the practical, co-operative action of mediation by student mediators. Such deliberative reflections are an instance of the continual exploration and critical examination of values-in-practice in contingent circumstances, which is integral to the open approach to knowledge (see Chapter 5) and expertise concerning which is not confined to senior school leaders. The point here is that participative initiatives such as peer mediation programmes are likely to encourage initiative and dispersed leadership where students are given recognised, institutional responsibilities to take and reflect upon decisions.

Thirdly, a concern with the institutional arrangements involves at the same time a concern with social justice. The degree to which the institutions for participation are open to all (professional educators, non-teaching staff, students, parents, and so on), without intended or unintended exclusions according to gender, social class, ethnic status and the like, is a test of both cultural and associational justice and is materially affected by the impact of distributive injustices. Developmental democracy disrupts hierarchy, as we saw in Chapter 2, from a particular direction. It gives institutional form to the positive and optimistic view of humanity, in which all have the spark of goodness and wisdom that enables and entitles everyone to have their say in the conduct of social life.

Another direction from which hierarchy is disrupted, overlapping with democracy, is a concern with the inequities of distribution and access to material resources and social capital. To be serious about greater democracy is to redress unacceptable distributive injustices (or at least make progress towards this). So, for example, institutional structures – distribution of resources, organisation of classes, behaviour policy, and so on – that address the needs of disadvantaged students are an essential contributor to redressing inequalities and enabling all students to develop literacy, numeracy and other skills that underpin educational progress and the capacity for participation. In addition, dispersal of leadership opportunities through the most effective forms of school councils, for example, can reduce student disaffection and exclusions from school (Inman with Burke 2002).

Beyond the school itself, the concern with distributive injustices implies a community-active approach which recognises the school's socio-cultural context and its impact on educational 'success' and 'failure' (Nixon et al. 1997). The idea of an emergent teacher professionalism, in the work of Nixon, Ranson and others in the 1990s, is bound up with schools engaging in community-based regeneration (Smyth 2001). The aim is to shift the structural conditions in which the school is operating through adopting an 'outward focus' concerned to empower the community, rather than retaining an exclusive 'inward focus', orientated to the institution and its values and educational priorities and in which the dominant concern is the school itself (P.A. Woods 2005). An outward focus aims to serve the learning needs of the community, which means not only educating within the school but also taking an 'outreach' approach serving the learning needs of the community wherever they are found.

> The task of educating individuals and groups in the community is defined as serving the wider purposes of empowering the community to regenerate its own social, economic and cultural development. From this perspective, boundaries are perceived as permeable in order to achieve the flexibility required to support learning where it is most appropriately located. (Martin et al. 1999: 63)

The importance of a community orientation has been taken up in the field of educational leadership. A 'radical reconceptualisation of the nature and purpose of such leadership is required', which in essence means a shift from 'institutional improvement to community transformation' (West-Burnham

2003: 6). West-Burnham's emphasis is on 'creating social capital rather than just improving classroom practice' (ibid.) and cites the relevance of Friere's 'emphasis on collegiality and consensual governance' (p. 7). However, despite this hint of radical possibilities, this approach by West-Burnham, and some others in the leadership field, does not engage in sustained social critique and questioning of power relations constituted in the wider political and economic context (Thrupp and Wilmott 2003). Yet a concern with collegiality and democratic leadership, framed within a developmental conception of democracy, implies the need to engage in just such a critique.

In light of the foregoing discussion, the institutional characteristics of democratic leadership that facilitates decisional rationality and authentic power sharing can be summarised as follows:

● *Dispersal of leadership.* Leadership roles and responsibilities are dispersed throughout the organisation, and leaders work to recognise and enhance this.

● *Decisional rights expressed through general and specific polities.* Participation includes recognised rights to take initiatives and exert influence within decision-making processes. This is not the same as consultation, but involves rights to vote, initiate or approve certain decisions and to hold power-holders to account and to apply sanctions. So, the practical manifestation of decisional rights includes: exercising democratically legitimated authority, that is, making or influencing decisions as an accountable post-holder (acting as a democratic positional leader); activating accountability processes, for example taking the initiative as an organisational or community member to elect or hold others to account (initiating a vote for example); taking the initiative in participatory, decision-making forums, by initiating debates or motions for example.

● *Dampening of power differences and distributive injustices.* Practical day-to-day power differences between individuals, hierarchically organised posts or stakeholder groups (education professionals, students, parents, and so on) are not allowed to undermine effective participation. Hence, developing and utilising the institutional arrangements involves a concern with the impact of distributive injustices, which includes an outward focus on inequalities in the school's external community.

Cultural

Part of the necessary firm framing is an affirmation, understood as a shared starting point, of what democracy and democratic leadership entail and the knowledge, ideas and values which underpin them. Implied here is a recapturing of a dominant discourse of performative, instrumental and market-led values and its reappropriation by a discourse of democracy. In short, some kind of shared vision of democratic aims and practice is needed.

Five points are integral to such a vision and its development. Firstly, it needs to enshrine the influencing ideas and ideals that underpin democracy and democratic leadership in the school. From the perspective of the developmental conception of democracy this encompasses:

- principles of democracy: freedom, equality, organic belonging, and substantive liberty;

- complementary, interacting dimensions of the practice of democratic leadership: ethical, decisional, discursive, and therapeutic rationalities.

These, expressed in some form or other, are guides to the practice of democratic leadership in a school. There are two things that it is particularly important that the vision should do. One is to reinforce the institutional provision for decisional rationality, discussed above, by affirming the rights and capacities of all those contributing to dispersed leadership. The other is to express and reinforce a commitment to aspiration to truth – the kernel of ethical rationality – as an essential component of the developmental conception of democracy. Aspiration to advance understanding, within an open approach to knowledge, needs to be embedded in the influencing ideas and ideals of the democratic school.

Secondly, understanding the oppositional nature of democratic leadership is crucial – the fact that it challenges dominant forces of instrumental rationality and the market. The implication is that schools, to take the journey towards democracy, need to develop an explicit orientation to the world, which expresses self-conscious adherence to certain ethical values and seeks to retain a degree of control and self-direction despite the relentless demands of rationalisation and the market economy. It needs to establish some distance from these structural forces, in the sense of Weber's notion of inner distance. Arguably, there is a dynamic at work assisting the creation of conditions for challenging the ascendancy of these forces. The persistence of uncommodified emotion alongside the dominance of instrumentality itself helps to develop a consciousness of that contradiction which serves to sharpen over time appreciation of the affective domain and its significance for our humanity. That consciousness and sensitivity to the affective can be enhanced by experience of free spaces built into the school structure.

But personal distancing from powerful alienating forces needs to be made a collective and historically-situated exercise. By recognising the challenge it is making to powerful structural forces as a community, a school makes inner distance a phenomenon that moves beyond a personal stance. The marketising reforms of the late 1980s and 1990s led some schools to adopt strategies specifically aimed at subverting the promotion of competition (Wallace 1998). Church schooling can be one form of institutional orientation, where the essential nature of, say, Catholic education is seen as antithetical to an ideology of market individualism (Pring 1996). Secular examples include the creative state school studied by Jeffrey and Woods (2003: 18) – the ethos of which encourages and supports everyone to adapt imaginatively to the tightly regulated national curriculum in England and to develop a 'resconstructed progressivism' – and the private, self-governing democratic ethos of Summerhill school founded by A.S. Neill (1990). In opposition to a highly regulated and bureaucratised education system in the USA, Central Park East Secondary School in New York follows an explicit set of principles that includes personalised learning and self-discovery by students. More than this, educators at the school have worked to elaborate what these principles mean. They conclude that the 'two qualities that seemed to define our ideal citizen were *empathy* and *scepticism*: the ability to see a situation from the eyes of another and the tendency to wonder about the validity of what we encountered' (Meier and Schwarz 1999: 34–5; original emphasis). In turn, identification of the importance of these two qualities is translated into ideas and values which inform the school's curriculum and assessment procedures. The point here is that articulated ideas and values (part of the school's culture) play a part in developing qualities necessary for the exercise of dispersed democratic leadership (these qualities are elaborated in Chapter 9).

This leads to a further, third point. The shared cultural context supportive of democracy includes the regulating ideals and theories of learning that guide the school. In other words, a conception of democratic pedagogies, borne out of the constellation of democratic principles and rationalities and the open approach to knowledge, needs to be seen as framing the approach to learning.

As with the democratic institutional arrangements, concerns with social justice thread themselves within democratic culture. Fourthly then, developing the ideas, values and vision that comprise the latter involves at the same time thinking through the impact of cultural injustices. The ideas and values given prominence in the school (its cultural structure) set the frame for action. These help to found strategic and day-to-day policy and practice. For example, for the principal creating a participatory school culture studied by Keyes et al. (1999), the goal of inclusion was non-negotiable and certain aims, such as including students with disabilities in general classrooms, were not open to critique. Also essential is giving high value to recognising inequalities and listening and being responsive to the differing needs of students and families in a culturally diverse society. More specifically, there are sets of background knowledge, awareness and orientations held by education professionals that need to be aligned with the specific communities and their experiences in which schools are embedded.

Two of the recommendations in Blair's (2001) UK study of black youth and school exclusion are highlighted here by way of illustration. Teachers, Blair concludes, need to be informed by an understanding of the 'historical relationship between black communities and the educational system in Britain' and of 'how racism operates and how various ethnic groups are differentially positioned within society' (p. 142). In addition, the school culture needs to acknowledge explicitly the importance of recognising that

> students might have particular problems relating to their backgrounds or families which require a sympathetic and compassionate approach rather than a condemnatory approach that puts students at risk by excluding them from school. (p. 142)

Equally, there is a need to be alert to changes. For example, concerning relations between families and schools, Martin (1999) challenges some assumptions, based on a study of parents of secondary school children in England. She suggests that less advantaged, working-class parents may be '"repositioning" themselves as more active partners in their children's education' (p. 60) and that there is evidence of Black, Asian and other minority ethnic groups being 'more positive [about involving themselves with their child's school] and surprisingly assertive given their traditional experience of marginalisation' (p. 60). In addition, Martin finds, more men appear to be taking an active role in their children's education, though the type of involvement may be influenced by gender, with men more likely to attend public meetings which represent the 'male' public sphere, than meetings about their own child which represent the 'female' sphere of home-school liaison.

Alertness to such trends and changes reinforces a fifth point, namely that the details of the school vision and strategies for its realisation are themselves developmental and will benefit from dispersed participation in their formulation and modification. A school vision in particular is often seen as emanating from the headteacher or school principal. An alternative approach is for the vision to emerge from a distributed process of creativity and debate in which everyone participates (Smith 2002). In the latter process, the headteacher still has a leading role – or an orchestrating role (see Chapter 10) – but its construction, and modification over time, are distributed and emergent rather than introduced as a phenomenon external to the school community. Indeed, an ongoing capacity for critical reflection on shared vision is of deep importance. There are inherent dangers with a vision that all are prompted to sign up to. There is a tension between the proper need for a shared sense of purpose and values, on the one hand, and facilitating democratic difference, questioning and dissent, on the other.

Here is one school principal in a democratic school:

> At every single meeting we have, the vision statement goes up first. We always recite it; it's our little mantra. It goes up on the overhead and sits on the table. It is what we believe. (Quoted in Blase and Blase 1999: 489).

Is this commendable collective reinforcement? Or is it indoctrination, antithetical to democratic principles? As Fullan (2001: 8) notes, groups can be powerful, which means 'they can be powerfully wrong' if they become dominated by 'groupthink' and an uncritical commitment to the leader and the dominant ideas. This applies equally to visions and strategies to create a more democratic school. Some continual check is needed to see whether 'organizational ethical dissonance' is developing, 'where the values reflected in the everyday style of leadership (values-in-use) drift away from the espoused commitment to higher order values integral to a public ethos' (Woods and Woods 2004: 667). Integral to democratic culture is the explicit valuing of the capability for constructive dissent and loyal opposition (see Chapter 9).

Social

Social patterns of interaction are part of the structural framing of any institution. These patterns – and the degree to which they cross and blur (if not eliminate) the traditional hierarchy – will be affected by the institutionalised boundaries in schools that separate teachers, students, parents and community. In particular, social interaction and communication are influenced by the extent of the blurred-status free space that characterises the institution's structure. Open, democratic relations that, because of presuppositions about human equality, are active across social boundaries of status and distinction place different expectations and requirements on relationships, as compared with social orders based on hierarchy (bureaucracy) or exchange (markets and networks).

Trust and mutual identification are particularly important dimensions of these relational expectations and requirements. Studies of shared leadership show that 'honest and on-going communication that builds high levels of mutual trust is centrally important for the establishment and durability of the collaboration' (Court 2003: 165). More widely, Lowndes argues that trust 'is the potential core of a new "governing code" for the twenty-first century' and that '[d]emocratic renewal, in its broadest sense, is contingent upon rebuilding trust in governance' (1999: 135). Trust, however, can take different forms. It can comprise just enough belief and faith in others to allow a bargain to be struck; or it can be a character of relations which grows out of interaction and learning over time and an indicator of socially developed personal affinities that emerge as part of a continually recreated identity of shared values and a conscious sense of community.

The point has been recognised in different terms by diverse writers who articulate a contrast between distinct types of relationship: Court emphasises high professional trust and responsibility (2004: 190), rather than linear accountability; Fielding advocates 'reciprocal responsibility' which 'requires a felt and binding mutuality' (2001: 700), rather than accountability which has the 'feel of bureaucratic rationality about it' (p. 699); and Raymond Williams argues for 'active mutual responsibility' (1963: 316) rather than enjoining people to be servants to others. Bottery (2003: 253–4) most clearly identifies the developmental nature of trust and the normative progression through types of trust and the relationships that go with these:

- calculative trust (a matter of personal calculation);

- practice trust (the product of repeated interaction);

- role trust (belief that occupants of a role, such as a doctor or teacher, are socialised into a set of values and commitments that can be relied upon);

- identificatory trust (deep-rooted interpersonal relationship characterised by 'a complex intertwining of personal thoughts, feeling and values' p. 253).

The idea of relationships based on a sense of service – as a contrast to calculative, bureaucratic or market-like relations – may seem attractive. But, if the relationship of leaders to others is not to be one reducible to bureaucratic rationality and manipulative transformation, the alternative of portraying it as one of service should be approached with some caution. Raymond Williams eschews it entirely as an appropriate goal. The problem is that service, in the sense of one set of persons (such as teachers) always knowing best and setting all the parameters of activity and purpose for another (such as students), may nurture dependence. Montessori, for example, argued in the early twentieth century:

> *He who is served is limited* in his independence. This concept will be the foundation of the dignity of the man of the future. 'I do not wish to be served, *because* I am not an impotent.' And this idea must be gained before men can feel themselves to be really free. (Montessori, quoted in Lawrence 1970: 328; original emphases)

The sense of potential for positive movement, from calculative trust to more developed and enriching levels of trust and relationship, accords well with the fundamental tenets of developmental democracy. The community that nourishes creative agents capable of shared democratic leadership requires 'a special mutual relationship between persons – a relationship at its lowest of esteem and respect, at its highest of affection and love' (Hughes 1951: 6). The nature of social relationships has implications for the degree to which associational justice is promoted and a dispersed pattern of democratic leadership nurtured. Antagonistic relationships between teachers and black students, for example, preclude effective inclusive participation (see Blair 2001: 33–4). Morwenna Griffiths explained what a positive social climate felt like from her own experience:

> Mr and Mrs Smith, who ran my junior school, taught me justice by example. No children in their classes were allowed to feel stupid or humiliated because they found work difficult. No children were allowed to feel arrogant – or bored – because they found work easy. I know: I was quick and sharp at maths … but slow and clumsy at art and craft … I remember the courtesy accorded to my classmates who were slower at grasping mathematics. (2003: 112)

At its widest, associational justice means that all stakeholders feel enabled and empowered to participate in dispersed leadership, as in Fielding's (1999) conception of radical collegiality. The point is that the quality of relationships predominant in the school creates a distinctive pattern and feel. Whatever the formal cultural and institutional position proclaiming inclusivity, the texture of actual, day-to-day relations will determine much about who is involved and who excluded. Certain basic qualities of social relationships are necessary to allow inclusive participation to develop, and this particularly includes expressions of care and respect as integral features of everyday relationships.

Conclusions: structural characteristics enshrining free space

Essential to understanding democratic leadership is an appreciation of the bivalent character of democracy, namely that it requires an organisational dynamic that allows for movement between relatively tight and relatively loose structural frameworks. The implication is that school leaders need to build into school structures a combination of free space, comprising independent zones and blurred status arenas, and firm framing. More specifically, a three-pronged approach is required which enshrines free space in a democratic frame. The components of this approach, summarised in Figure 8.1, constitute the main structural characteristics for attention in creating and sustaining democratic leadership.

Institutional:
specific entitlements, roles and forums that facilitate:
• dispersal of leadership
• decisional rights
• dampening of power differences and distributive injustices
Cultural:
shared vision of democracy which includes:
• articulation of democratic principles and rationalities
• affirmation of rights and capacities of all to contribute to dispersed leadership
• commitment to advancing understanding within open approach to knowledge
• explicit ethical stance that establishes distance from the structural forces of instrumental rationality and the market
• a conception of democratic pedagogies
• awareness of and challenge to cultural injustices
• recognition that the vision itself is developmental, participative and requires ongoing critical reflection which values constructive dissent
Social:
• a texture of relations which expresses trust and mutual responsibility, care and respect, founded in deep-rooted interpersonal relationships

---

Figure 8.1: Creating and sustaining democratic leadership – structural characteristics

Firstly, such an approach builds an institutional structure which provides specific entitlements, roles and forums that encourage power sharing. These need to facilitate:

• dispersal of leadership;

• decisional rights (expressed through general and specific polities) which include: exercising democratically legitimated authority, activating accountability processes, and taking the initiative in participatory, decision-making forums;

* dampening of power differences and distributive injustices.

Secondly, it creates a cultural structure that comprises a shared vision of democratic aims and practice. The vision incorporates:

* articulation of the principles of democracy (freedom, equality, organic belonging, and substantive liberty) and complementary, interacting dimensions of the practice of democratic leadership (ethical, decisional, discursive, and therapeutic rationalities), including in particular: affirmation of the rights and capacities of all to contribute to dispersed leadership and expression and reinforcement of a commitment to aspiration to truth (the kernel of ethical rationality), in the sense of advancing understanding, within an open approach to knowledge;

* a self-conscious orientation to the world, that aspires to ethical values and self-direction in the context of relentless demands of rationalisation and the market economy;

* a conception of democratic pedagogies;

* awareness of and challenge to cultural injustices in the specific context of the school;

* recognition that the vision itself is developmental, will benefit from dispersed participation and requires ongoing critical reflection which values constructive dissent.

The third prong of this approach is to create a social structure that is characterised by a texture of day-to-day relations which expresses or grows towards identificatory trust and a sense of mutual responsibility, care and respect, founded in deep-rooted interpersonal relationships.

Notes

1 *Oxford Companion to Philosophy*, Oxford University Press, 1995 (from website, www.xrefer.com/entry/552724). See also Meszaros's (1970: 162–8) discussion of Marx's notion of 'self-mediation'.

9 Capabilities and skills for democratic leadership

It is worth repeating that the practice of distributed and democratic leadership is not limited to those in formal positions of leadership at the apex of a school hierarchy – headteachers and principals, and other senior school managers. It extends to all who contribute to leadership as an organisational force emergent from collective and interactive effort. This means everyone in the school community who exercises initiative which influences other people, stimulates action, change and a sense of direction, and is successful to some degree in the way intended – in other words, all who share in the circulation of initiative. Democratic leadership by its nature is dispersed, involving a multiplicity of people contributing actively and consciously to organisational leadership.

Having said that, senior positional leaders are likely to have an important, often decisive role in creating and sustaining the conditions for dispersed, democratic leadership in a school. That being so, we come to a fundamental issue. Is democratic participation a gift to be handed over (or retained at will) by positional leaders? Is it an entitlement or a human potential to be assumed, demanded and perhaps in the end taken by those lower in the hierarchy – the result of a 'bottom-up' initiative (Woods et al. 2004)? In practice, the two directions of approach are likely to interact and complement each other.

Either way, there is a great deal to take on if an organisation is to take a democratic turn. A number of motives or orientations can lead to resistance to democratic leadership and a more democratic culture: self-interest (the power-holder who wants to maintain the status quo or the power-deficient who wants to remain free from additional responsibility); habits of deference; belief in the superior efficiency of hierarchy and governance by command and control; apathy; and reasoned scepticism.[1] Each of these needs to be shifted towards or more effectively balanced by a counterweight:

self-interest	by	collective responsibility
deference	by	assertiveness
belief in hierarchy	by	belief in collegiality
apathy	by	activism
reasoned scepticism	by	reasoned confidence in democratic leadership

The role of dispersed leaders – all those contributing to leadership outside the senior formal position – and the conditions for active circulation of leadership are crucial. Resistance is overcome by knowing the possibilities (and being realistic about these), seeing the potential for the right conditions to be introduced and developed in ones own organisational context, and nurturing the necessary capabilities and skills amongst leaders and would-be leaders.

Surowiecki (2004: 10) argues that the conditions necessary to facilitate what he calls the *wisdom of crowds* are:

- *diversity of opinion*: each person should have some private information, even if it is his or her own interpretation of what is generally known about an issue;

- *independence*: each person's opinion should not be determined by those around them;

- *decentralisation*: each person has his or her own local knowledge of the question or issue;

- *aggregation*: there needs to be some means for turning private judgements into a collective decision. (This is the domain of structures and processes discussed in the previous chapter.)

Nurturing of these sorts of conditions has implications for both formal and informal leaders. Research has pointed to the importance of senior figures relinquishing and withdrawing from their power and authority (Blase and Blase 1999; Hallinger and Kantamara 2000). This is especially important in organisations and cultures where there is a tradition of deference, which necessitates 'disarmament' strategies designed to reduce the power distance between senior leaders and their constituencies (Hallinger and Kantamara 2000: 200). Blase and Blase suggest that backing off means that school leaders in positions of formal authority act in specific ways that leave space for teachers 'to share power, make decisions and take responsibility for their decisions' (1999: 483). Ways of backing off found by Blase and Blase involve school leaders:

- extracting themselves from decision-making processes to a great extent;

- avoiding monitoring teachers and contradicting their decisions;

* encouraging teachers to participate voluntarily in committee and task-force work;

* encouraging teachers to represent the school at regional meetings of shared-governance schools;[2]

* encouraging openness to risk and experimentation;

* coming to terms with the fact that some may view a leader who backs off as weak.

Fundamentally, what is required is 'shedding status' (Trafford 2003: 64); and not only amongst professional educators, but also between teachers and students. A headteacher who worked to develop a democratic school over many years observed:

> When we retreat behind our status and keep an emotional, if not physical, distance from them, our pupils are by no means convinced that we like them. Nor are they sure that we are willing to be approached if they are worried or need help. So while on the grand occasion status may be used positively, most of the time we teachers need to abandon the dais (whether it's a real or imaginary one) and get down to their level. (Trafford 2003: 66)

Backing away from power is not easy, and there are tensions and contradictions bound up with such an approach. The key position of the headteacher or principal carries responsibilities, so that he or she is required to take a leading role to bring about and sustain change. This may be done in subtle ways (as will be discussed in Chapter 10). But holding back from contradicting teachers and from continually checking up on them is not the same as a *laissez-faire* approach which ignores poor teaching. Two-way communication in a climate of high trust and reciprocal responsibility has to be the aim, which enables active sharing and identification of both weaknesses and strengths by staff at all levels, transparent processes for collegial support and, if necessary, tough action where a colleague's contribution warrants this.

For the multiplicity of leaders in a democratic community, there needs to be a readiness, which has to be cultivated, to seek and take the initiative. It also requires a preparedness to shoulder responsibility for decisions taken collectively. Indeed, leadership by senior leaders, and all who contribute to emergent, distributed leadership which is involved in creating and nurturing democratic schooling, requires a variety of capabilities and skills. These have a personal dimension, since they are rooted in individuals. They also have a collective dimension in that they are more than the sum of the parts and have greater power in a context of mutually reinforcing and complementary expertise and experience. These key capabilities and skills are out-lined here.

Status adaptability: shedding/taking status as appropriate. As noted, shed-ding status – and thus having a capacity to back away from fixed status and power hierarchies – is integral to changes that aim to forge a more dispersed and democratic form of leadership. The other side of the coin concerns those who lack status and power. Their challenge is to take to themselves a new status and opportunities which invite them to be initiative-takers and to exercise influence in a more equal set of relationships. The idea of status adaptability is intended to capture both sides of the coin. Indeed, the same person may be required to shed status in one context (a teacher in a class-room for example) and take status in another (that same teacher in a meeting with senior school leaders). Even the most radical form of systemic change – abolition of hierarchy and of authority roles such as headteacher or principal – may require similar kinds of status adaptability where infor-mal status and power differences emerge.

Communicative virtues.[3] A key issue is 'how to listen to and talk with each other constructively in situations of difference and disagreement over values, educational philosophies or practices' (Court 2003: 165). For princi-pals, the need is to establish open communication 'by listening, by actively encouraging input and feedback (including criticism of self and programs), by making themselves available for interaction and discussion … and by recognizing and praising teachers' (Blase and Blase 1999: 484). Commu-nicative virtues can be expressed as a series of requirements on all partici-pants in discursive rationality which are important in enabling constructive and open exchange:[4]

- be prepared to express a view;
- be as clear as possible;
- be honest and transparent;
- be tolerant;
- be patient;
- be willing to take criticism;
- practice self-restraint;
- be willing to re-examine one's presuppositions and basic views.

The more these are practised and reinforced, the more a culture is forged where these become the expectation and in which organisational members are invited to participate, using and personalising these norms as their own communicative virtues. They create an organisational property of, to use Sidorkin's term, 'civility', that is 'institutionalised dialogue' (1999: 129).

Independence. Independence of mind and the confidence to criticise and challenge are essential. Teachers and others 'should be proactive about asserting themselves when democratic principal leadership does not occur' (Reitzug and O'Hair 2002: 139). But it goes further than voicing concerns about departures from democratic leadership. The policy, organisational and educational decisions of positional leaders, as well as their conduct, cannot be above questioning and challenge. This involves preparedness to express what Grint (2005) refers to as 'constructive dissent'. It means having a willingness and confidence to point out the errors of senior leaders. It requires subordinates 'to remain committed to the goals of the community or organization whilst simultaneously retaining their spirit of independence from the whims of their leaders' (op. cit.: 45). This demands a capacity to maintain a 'paradoxical combination of commitment and independence' (ibid.). It also means unlearning the habits of hierarchy that involve an ingrained deference to authority (one of the obstacles to democratic leadership highlighted in Chapter 7). Crucially too, of course, it demands a capacity on the part of senior leaders to take, respect and seriously consider dissent without retreating behind their status (in other words, status adaptability). One way that senior leaders may approach this is to value within the school community the individual voice or collectivity of voices which act 'as a "loyal opposition"' (Robertson and Webber 2002: 547) to the majority and/or to the school's senior authority figures.

Knowledge and understanding of democratic principles and practices. Without this, how can people create and nurture a democratic community within which they are active leaders? Reitzug and O'Hair highlight the importance of access to knowledge and to coaching and support which enables 'teachers and other educators to learn about and implement practices that reflect the beliefs of their democratic community' (2002: 139). Participation in the development of a school's shared vision of democratic aims and practice (which forms part of the institution's cultural structure), and ongoing critical reflection about it, are themselves opportunities for learning about democratic leadership.

Skills in developing and sustaining community. The particular texture of day-to-day relations which expresses identificatory trust and a sense of mutual responsibility, care and respect and is characteristic of the social structure discussed in Chapter 8, does not emerge unbidden, without the efforts of individuals. Developing a community spirit of mutual concern and identification is a continual task that draws on individual capabilities and skills. Equally, the community acts upon the individual. The developmental, democratic form of community constitutes an environment that encourages individuality in a supportive context. Hence, it can be argued

that being capable of developing a community spirit is of the most fundamental importance because 'it is necessary in order to develop creative personalities in small life-sustaining communities, and to weld such
communities into larger ones' (Hughes 1951: 7).

Respect. Respect for others is a foundation for a democratic community
and the exercise of democratic leadership, and a dimension of cultural
justice. The feeling to which this refers is, however, rather more profound
than the term 'respect' perhaps implies. Bertrand Russell refers to *reverence*
for others (Hughes 1951: 45), which begins to convey more appropriately
the deep-seated consideration and esteem that is given to the life of the
other person – indeed, to each of the lives and personalities that make up
the organisational community. The depersonalised world analysed by
Weber (see Chapter 4) has the merit of sharpening understanding of the significance of personality: not personality as a bundle of assorted passions
and emotions triggered by biological stimuli and subjective whims, but personality as the unique being who has the potential, through an inner distance from depersonalised and depersonalising pressures, for discovery and
creation of the profoundest meaning (and hence for ethical rationality).
Reverence for others and for this endlessly repeated potential in unique
individuals is not strictly a capability or skill. Its cultivation, however, is of
fundamental importance.

Capacity for 'profound participation'.[5] This is about the extent to which
people's full awareness and self is engaged. It is about not allowing ones
voice to be constructed solely by the role one occupies and the dominant
expectations of that organisational positioning. The latter is best described
as 'functional participation', which describes a more formalised engagement as a member of a group, in other words, as a particular role holder.
Nor is profound participation equivalent to emotionalism – giving unfettered expression to feelings, which puts emotion in control and is incon-
sistent with positive freedom. Rather, it is about recognising and
incorporating in one's self as participant, and in one's understanding of
others, the differences that make the individual personality. In the terms of
critical humanism, in order to be authentic, voices need to be based on an
understanding of 'the bedrock of personal experience and feeling on which
personalities are formed' (Nemiroff 1992: 88). Or to put it another way, we
speak as a person, not simply as a role-holder or member of a socio-cultural
group (women, Blacks, working class, and so on). The process of profound
participation, as an element of practical social engagement, is returned to
in Chapter 10.

Critical reflection on inner potential and outer context. The responsibility
placed on individuals increases with the success of dispersing democratic
leadership. Each is called upon to contribute to the everyday creation of the
institutional, cultural and social structures of the school and, in particular, to

forging a pattern of day-to-day relationships that are not dominated by calculative trust but value mutual responsibility and care. There is a *personal* responsibility to help create a texture of relations which possesses human warmth (Woods 2001). But this is not to say that an ostrich-like withdrawal from hard-headed recognition of the organisational and social contexts that intrude into the personal and interpersonal aspects of organisational life is in order. Many educational professionals under pressures of globalisation 'retreat to the parochial and insular, in the hope that at this level, true meaning, personal identity, enriching relationships can be found ... Yet ignoring the powerful doesn't make them go away' (Bottery 2004: 14). Nemiroff (1992: 89), from a perspective of critical humanism, suggests a set of questions that learners should ask themselves. I suggest that Nemiroff's questions (listed below) apply to adult school leaders too, as a means of focusing on the dialectical relationship between inner potential and outer context:

- Who am I?

- What have been the most formative factors in my development?

- Which of these are individual and which are systemic?

- How do I feel when I have been diminished by a person or a situation?

- What actions and choices can be impelled by specific feelings?

- By whose criteria am I making my value judgements? If they are not mine, why am I appropriating them?

- In whose interests am I acting, and whose 'voices' are telling me what to do?

- What are my feelings about countering authority, and where do they come from?

- What part of me craves emancipation, and how does this feel?

Cultivation of 'power with'. The democratic leader inspires co-operation and creates a group power rather than cultivating personal power. The idea of promoting 'power with', rather than 'power over' is advanced from a feminist perspective (see, for example, Blackmore 1999; Grace 2001). This is a redefining of power as 'power through and with others – shared leadership – "being at the centre of the spokes of a wheel rather than out in front pulling the wagon"' (Blackmore 1999: 161). It goes back to earlier advocates of democratic leadership in education such as Hughes (1951: 38). Advancing 'power with' is about developing a collective and mutually supportive striving for what is good and right, or the nearest we can get to it by practising ethical and discursive rationality.

The right conclusion is not what [the democratic leader] demands; it is not always what the majority demands; it is what the situation demands, and this becomes clear only in the course of discussions – an essential educative process for leaders, majorities and minorities alike. (op. cit.: 38–9).

Conflict handling. The capacity to handle and resolve conflicts is integral to distributed leadership (Bennett et al. 2003a). This requires avoidance of personal hostility and can benefit from provision of training in conflict management (Blase and Blase 1999). There is a link here with peer mediation of student conflicts. Certain individual skills are necessary for peer mediation, such as skills in affirmation, communication, co-operation and knowledge and understanding of problem solving (Clough and Holden 2002). But personal capacities are not in themselves sufficient, nor are they constituted and expressed independently of the organisational context. How peer mediation is set up gives and encourages or, conversely, withholds opportunities to exercise initiative and leadership, and to learn how to do this. It can enable groups of students to work together and develop their own protocols and ways of working, or can fail to offer such opportunities, depending on how schemes are set up and operated (Bickmore 2001). The message is that student leaders have to be given both support and space to exercise control. As a trainer of peer mediators in the UK explained

> In many of the schools in which I have encountered peer mediation schemes, they appear to have been very successful in both developing the skills of those trained and in having an impact on reducing instances of destructive conflict. However, this has only been the case in schools prepared to change their school organisation and culture rather than schools who specifically want to change the behaviour of a problem class. (Quoted in Clough and Holden 2002: 29)

The trainer goes on to conclude that peer mediation:

> has to be part of a whole school initiative, where all staff are prepared to endorse the scheme and allow pupils opportunities to regulate their own behaviour. (p. 29)

In other words, participatory approaches to conflict resolution are less successful where the concern is an immediate, instrumental one: adopt technique x in order to eliminate problem y. The general point applies to staff and other stakeholders such as parents, since divergences of interest and the potential for clashes of views, groups and personalities are ubiquitous and conflicts can occur within and between any of a school's stakeholder groups. Conflict handling skills and capabilities have to be developed as part of an organisational culture which accepts and addresses the challenge of conflicts that arise from these divergences and clashes.

Conclusions: capabilities, skills and attitudes

The main capabilities, skills and attitudes for attention in creating and sustaining democratic leadership are summarised in Figure 9.1.

Where they coalesce most effectively, the combined effect of these personal characteristics is to reinforce the shedding of status and reduction of power differences and to diminish the potency of the motivations and orientations that encourage resistance to democratic leadership. However, they do not develop as free-standing variables. Rather, they are generated, flourish and exert an influence through their dialectical relationship with the structural conditions for democratic leadership and the day-to-day practical engagement as democratic leaders. It is to this practical engagement we now turn.

Capabilities and skills:
- status adaptability: shedding or taking status as appropriate
- communicative virtues
- independence
- knowledge and understanding of democratic principles and practices
- skills in developing and sustaining community
- respect
- capacity for profound participation
- critical reflection on inner potential and outer context
- cultivation of 'power with'
- conflict handling

Receptive attitudes:
- collective responsibility
- assertiveness
- belief in collegiality
- activism
- reasoned confidence in democratic leadership

Figure 9.1: Creating and sustaining democratic leadership – capabilities, skills and attitudes

Notes

1 See Figure 7.1, Chapter 7.
2 The schools of the principals studied by Blase and Blase were members of the League of Professional Schools in the USA, the purpose of which is to support the establishment of representative, democratic decision-making structures.
3 The phrase is taken from Ryan (2002: 996), referring to Burbules (1993).
4 This list draws from work by Blase and Blase (1999), Burbules (1993), Court (2003) and Ryan (2002).
5 In her work on teachers, Cooper (2003) has developed the concepts of functional empathy (focused on the group) and profound empathy (focused on an individual). The idea of profound participation was stimulated by these ideas.

10 *Complexities and demands of practice*

The developmental conception of democracy has implications for how we understand the practice of democratic leadership. This chapter summarises implications for the exercise of democratic leadership, gleaned from the earlier, theoretical chapters, then addresses further issues concerning its practice.

Implications so far

It is possible to extricate from the theoretical discussion of democracy and democratic practice key implications for the exercise of democratic leadership.[1] Firstly, democratic leadership involves practice of democratic rationalities, namely: engaging in the search for common human good (ethical); exercising and facilitating deliberation and dialogic democracy (discursive); dispersing leadership, exercising and being subject to accountability, and taking up and respecting recognised rights to participate in decision making (decisional); and contributing to leaders' own and others' growth towards human potential (therapeutic).

Secondly, it involves the encouragement of benign creativity, particularly by creating the conditions which

- are conducive to appreciation of emotional senses and navigational feelings;

- encourage recognition of the contradiction within the person in contemporary society between these and the dominant 'steel shell' of instrumental rationality;

- help to transform the dominant instrumental rationality into a critical but non-dominating analytical rationality;

- encourage reintegration of human capacities through the development, application and recombination of affective capacities with a complementary analytical rationality.

Thirdly, democratic leadership opens boundaries of participation and champions inclusion based on human status (the consequence of a fundamental valuing of each person's humanistic potential). Fourthly, it values autonomy of the person as an inherent good and creative space as necessary for human creativity and flourishing. Fifthly, democratic leadership encourages a critical humanism which, whilst valuing each person's humanistic potential, promotes awareness and understanding of the 'hard' realities of modernity. Finally, it encourages an open approach to knowledge, which advances learning through

- a continual dialectical movement between a rationalist epistemology (which views certain truths as known) and a critical epistemology (which views all conceptions – facts, theories and values – as perpetually open to critique);
- the creative application of tentative knowledges in practical action.

Further implications

More, however, needs to be understood about the practice of democratic leadership and the implications of the richness and demands of the democratic ideal, if it is to have a chance of being nurtured in the everyday life of schools.

Engaging in democratic leadership in a school that aspires to developmental democracy implies involvement as a person in a profound sense. It requires an authentic involvement, in the sense of commitment and direction that are guided by deeply embedded navigational feelings. This is illustrated by the headteacher (Sue) of a school studied by Jeffrey and Woods which prides itself on creativity and collaborative working:

> In many ways, [the school] is an expression of Sue's self ... Despite the constraints and opposing pressures, teachers can engage with the curriculum at a deep personal level. Sue shows that this can apply to the school itself ... it provides opportunities to 'be yourself', to 'be whole' and to 'be natural'. (2003: 125)

This sort of leadership is characterised by profound participation, which involves fostering and engaging in democratic leadership both as a role holder and as an individual, the capacity for which was highlighted in the discussion of capabilities and skills (see Chapter 9). Participation as an individual means each positional and dispersed leader engaging in leadership as a personality who has the potential for discovery and creation of the profoundest meaning.

Democratic leadership calls for benign creativity and self-transcendence. The actions of this kind of leadership are not orientated solely to the whims and interests of the person. Rather, they are orientated to the development of the inner person and a conception of what is of enduring worth. Profound participation aspires to engagement which draws on navigational feelings that orientate action to ideals of the good and the right. Lecturing on democratic leadership in the years immediately following the Second World War, Hughes (1951: 16) argued that integral to being a democratic leader are the tasks of enabling oneself and others to

- develop a harmonious personality;

- co-operate in the creation of friendships and communities;

- take a share 'however humble, in the creation of truth, beauty and goodness'.

The latter phrasing may sound anachronistic in the context of what some see as post-modern society. The words, however, are ways of representing and articulating deeply important areas of life that sometimes are often dimly perceived among the pressures of everyday living. Thinking about them reminds us as well that profound participation does not rely only on inner personal strength and resources. Structural supports are important too. Hence, the articulation of ideals is an important function of the cultural structure of the school (see Chapter 8), in particular articulation of the democratic principles of freedom, equality, organic belonging, and substantive liberty and commitment to truth in the sense of advancing understanding within an open approach to knowledge. These linguistic abstractions are important symbols which constitute meaning-laden resources for building and sustaining identity and helping to give direction to social action. In this way they act as identity orientations (P. A. Woods 2003). They are part of the organisational cultural capital on which positional and dispersed leaders can draw. Such expressions are powerful orientating symbols to ideals that give democracy, in its developmental vision, supervening value and meaning which demand educational attention.[2] Moreover, as shared symbols with collective support, they have the potential to sharpen perceptions of enduring values dimmed by everyday pressures.

Hughes's identification of democratic leadership with enabling, as a leader, both oneself and others to aspire to these elevated aims echoes ethically transforming leadership (see Chapter 3). It draws attention back to one of the main elements of ethically transforming leadership which involves mutual raising of ethical aspirations and conduct (G.J. Woods 2003). An overlapping proposition of democratic and ethically transforming leadership is that sensitivity and insight on ethical issues are not the exclusive preserve of senior positional leaders, but that working to orientate everyday action to the highest values and ideals is the responsibility and potential of positional and dispersed leaders. To put it another way, all those involved in leadership need to engage in ethical rationality both because they have something to contribute and because they may benefit and learn from it in terms of their own ethical orientation and conduct.

The highest values and ideals are capable of becoming components of practical, day-to-day engagement as democratic leaders. Blase and Blase (1999), in their study of principals of US schools exemplifying shared governance (involving participation and empowerment of teaching and other staff, parents and students), found that the inner experience of democratic leadership was significant amongst these principals. For some principals, shared governance was a spiritual experience that allowed them to express their deepest values and beliefs. Democratic leadership seeks to enact the genuine re-enchantment of labour, which is the product of the nurturing and appreciation of navigational feelings. Evidence that self-transcending leadership of the sort integral to democratic leadership is not simply 'pie in the sky' comes from research with headteachers in England which suggests that 'many leaders are already nourished by a sense of connectivity and profound spiritual awareness' (G.J. Woods 2005). Profound participation that draws on these sorts of resources is an essential component of ethical rationality.

On its own, a conviction that one is pursuing the profoundest values is no guarantee that this is actually the case. Nor is it a guarantee of a commitment to authentic democracy. The rhetoric of values can easily be wrapped around the task of securing the commitment of teachers, students and parents to working creatively towards organisational goals that owe more to the spur to succeed in a performance culture than genuine educational needs.

Appeals to such rhetoric can be used by clever leaders in both interpersonal forms of pseudo-participation (involving private persuasion) and adversarial forms of pseudo-participation (involving public performances of persuasion).[3] Hence, it has to be consistently emphasised that profound participation and ethical rationality need to be complemented by the critical engagement of others who exercise decisional rights and engage in a dynamic, questioning discursive rationality. Otherwise there is a danger of courting reliance on the heroic leader's characteristic of transformational leadership. Many studies present evidence that promotion of democratic or dispersed leadership emanates from the efforts of a strong or charismatic leader (Blase and Blase 1999; Campbell et al. 2003; Gold et al. 2002; Keyes et al. 1999; Reitzug and O'Hair 2002; Woods et al. 2004). However, I want to phrase this point slightly differently. It can be expressed in a more appropriate way as follows: development and sustenance of a more participatory culture requires some form of lead agency, that is, initiative and actions which play a decisive role in setting the possibilities and guiding principles, and in enabling resources (of legitimacy as well as material resources) to be made available to others. This often, but not always, emanates from those in leadership positions possessing senior institutional authority.

Lead agency need not be, and usually should not be, impositional but facilitative (Reitzug and O'Hair 2002). For the development of dispersed democratic leadership, it needs to be complementary to and supportive of 'bottom-up' initiative (Woods et al. 2004) and hence of leadership diffused throughout the formal hierarchy. The heroic figure of transformational leadership is not the ideal form that lead agency should take. Indeed, lead agency can be exercised by a group working in concert, supporting, testing and energising each other.

Moreover, the style of lead agency can appropriately be closer to Wallace's (2003) idea of orchestration, which is more in touch with the subtleties and nuances of complex organisations. Orchestration is about steering the complex change process, often at a distance from the 'sharp end' of activity. It is about keeping change on course during the long haul and includes (p. 24):

- maintaining momentum;

- monitoring others' practice relating to the change;

- channelling their agency in the desired direction through encouragement and incentive, and if necessary corrective action.

Wallace sees this as a realistic way of coping with educational visions that in a centralised education system emanate from politicians and of ameliorating and accepting ambiguity. It is a way, also, of educational leaders enacting a 'mildly subversive practical agenda' (p. 28) and importing to increasingly regulated school systems an element of discretionary leadership (as opposed to unthinking execution of central mandates). The essential idea of orchestration – accepting that school leaders have modest yet still significant potential to effect discretionary change – has relevance to advancing a vision of democratic schooling. Change towards democratic principles and practice in the school is not necessarily, or always desirably, a radical jump following the visionary leader. Rather, it requires a steady encouragement and spreading of institutional, cultural and social patterns that over time advance – unsteadily, with setbacks and unintended consequences always possible – towards the ideal.

The orchestrating approach stands a better chance of creating effective democracy. The orchestrating leader or leaders use the resources at their disposal to initiate change, prompt and maintain progress and check aberrations along the way. Effective leadership is often quiet leadership which builds 'slowly, carefully and collectively' (Mintzberg et al. 2002: 71, quoted in Glatter 2004). Quiet leaders bring about long-term change through a combination of virtues which include restraint, humility, tenacity and 'intense professional will' (Fullan 2003: 70).

The quiet, orchestrated approach can be seen amongst the principals studied by Blase and Blase (1999). Moves to greater democratic governance generally began by the principals 'planting and nurturing' the seeds of the idea, then in the early days of its implementation planning carefully 'the selection, rotation and inclusion' of the membership of decision making structures such as schools councils, liaison groups and task forces (p. 483). Whilst the principal backed a vision for change, the process was 'ongoing and evolutionary' (p. 487). Over time, in line with democratic principles, the locus of power to appoint disperses, by making appointments through election, letting go and standing back from power and authority and shedding status.

The point about orchestration and quiet leadership is that they highlight the degree to which sharing leadership is about small actions as much as the big change. Small actions, by senior positional and dispersed leaders, eventually make a big difference through the organisational footprints that accumulate and which come to have an enduring structural presence. In other words, the institutional framework, cultural ideas and ideals and social patterns of a school emerge from personal and collective engagement. People draw their resources for action from the given structure they inhabit at any one point in time and apply their own evaluations and creative capabilities. This sort of creative engagement, which might mean a small alteration to a pattern of behaviour or relationship or a larger innovation such as institutionalising free space for staff and students, both utilises and changes the given structural context (in the way suggested by the trialectic framework in the Introduction). The outcome of that creative engagement in turn becomes a structural resource for others. This process Holland et al. (1998) refer to as 'microgenesis'. New actions which are repeated and replicated create a pattern, which forms a new part of the structure.

Creative engagement clearly may be motivated by a variety of reasons, which include organisational or self interests (to increase efficiency or to make one's own life easier for example). Democratisation can benefit from a belief that it will advance personal or group interests (and be diverted or obstructed for similar reasons, as discussed in Chapter 7). Accordingly, instrumental arguments that democratic leadership will aid motivation and organisational capacity have an appeal for those leaders concerned principally about organisational performance. However, developmental democracy by its nature implies movement from this kind of instrumental approach – which in the practical world has its place – towards engagement rooted in a profound participation orientated to ideals and navigational feelings.

In Morwenna Griffith's (2003) book on social justice, Melanie Walker reflects on her experience of being brought up in South Africa and of the struggle against apartheid. She responds to Griffith's suggestion that a better metaphor than that of the heroic leader is Aesop's fable of the mice freeing the lion.

> While the work started with the action of one mouse, and then required collaboration, it was action towards a particular end, freedom. So that seems to be another important lesson (or moral) to draw from this story … Only when we stitch the pieces (our actions) together to make a quilt do the patterns emerge and transform the pieces into something new; we need to know what we are trying to make and to be able to judge whether we have made it well. (Melanie Walker, in Griffiths 2003: 123)

Working towards an end in mind – such as freedom – is one way of proceeding. It might be taken from this, however, that setting the goal means that social change can be ordered in the same way as creating a product, like a quilt. In fact, there is also a great deal of discovery and improvisation. In particular, generating and applying values through practical action in contingent circumstances, which is integral to the open approach to knowledge, is, as Joas suggests, a creative exercise that is not rule-bound and guaranteed to bring about certain ends.

Let us consider the student mediators studied by Bickmore (2001) as an example. They are engaged in seeking solutions to conflicts and finding ways of reconciling discordant actions and views. Where peer mediation was most comprehensively implemented, they were treated as leaders, taking initiatives and making decisions 'about how to interpret and adapt the mediation process in their community/cultural context and how to confront some important problems in their communities, such as school attendance and violence' (Bickmore 2001: 157). They were contributing, in effect, to the democratic leadership of their school and to the changing structure and culture of the school – in small, creative ways (microgenesis). Effective dispersal of democratic leadership involves conscious participation in microgenesis.

What is evident here is that we are talking about the broad curriculum of the school, understood as everything that is experienced and learnt by students in their schooling. Democratic pedagogies are as much about this broad curriculum as the teaching in the classroom (which became clear in the discussion in Chapter 6). The influence of positional school leaders, as well as the process and effects of dispersed leadership, are inherently part of the broad curriculum of the school and its pedagogy. The daily social engagement by dispersed leaders creates the texture of social relations that forms trust and mutual responsibility and comprises the broad democratic pedagogy which communicates the broad curriculum.

This texture is created by cumulative actions, particularly what might be termed the 'gifts and injuries' involved in engagement. Simmel, in an examination of human gratitude, discussed reciprocity where there is social exchange over time but no external enforcement on one party to return in equivalent terms that which is given by another (in other words, reciprocity where there is no contractual, calculative relationship). What underpins this process of unforced exchange is not utilitarian calculation nor a passing rush of goodwill on receipt of that which is given, but an enduring and deeply embedded feeling that Simmel termed 'gratitude'. Gifts, which may be material or otherwise (affection, intellectual help and so on), are so characteristic of and necessary to social life that the effect of gratitude can be described as the 'moral memory' of humankind (Simmel 1964: 388). It is the inner consequence of a tacit awareness that everyday living is dependent on social gifts, namely giving in numerous small and sometimes big ways without expectation of immediate, or sometimes any, return. The obverse of these sorts of gifts – which is not mentioned by Simmel – is injury: namely, all those ways, both physical and otherwise, by which people hurt or demean others.

Gifts and injuries are infinitely variable and evident in the everyday life of education at all levels. They include the encouragements and unnecessary pain highlighted by Knight (2001).[4] They are actions which through microgenesis create the intangible but real ethos of a school. This headteacher explains his view on what needs to be given in the everyday interaction with students: respect, time and attention.

> What's important, in fact I tell my staff – they hate me for it – you live your life very comfortably without working knowledge of Adam's law. OK, you need Adam's law for GCSE ... but you don't need it to live your life. I want these kids in 20 years time to look back and say, hey that wasn't a bad school, that head spoke to me and he was quite a reasonable person and I was enriched by that experience ... I believe that when you're 14, when you're 15, when you're 16, your paper qualifications are the least important aspect of what you experienced in a school and it's about the way people treated you, the way people spoke to you, the way people helped you cope with the fact you'd been abused, the way that people helped you cope with the alienation that comes because there is a lot of social and emotional deprivation here. (Secondary school headteacher)[5]

Students are acutely sensitive to this and to the obverse – injury, in the form of a sense of indifference and disengagement conveyed by teachers for example. That sensitivity is illustrated by this student:

> They [the teachers] all don't want to be here and you know they don't want to be here and they don't like this school. And you just know that, and you just pick it up. 'I'd rather be anywhere than here, I'd rather be in Morocco, but I'm just going to be here because I've got to earn some money.' And you know there are some teachers which have got a genuine love for the kids, Miss M sometimes, Miss A ... (Secondary school student)[6]

Students are not just subject *to* the school and teachers either. Through their actions and interactions (absenteeism, deviance, commitment to learning and so on), they are also 'world (school) builders' (Riseborough 1985: 262). Students are capable of subjecting teachers to what Riseborough terms being 'warrened' (p. 261), that is, being undermined psychologically – in other words, to small but telling injuries. Equally, they can build up and support teachers and school leaders through myriad, small positive actions.

The replacement of a culture of injury (shouting at students, putting people in their place down a sharp hierarchy of status and power, rebuffing parental requests for involvement) with one of giving is how the headteacher's strategy can be interpreted in another study by Riseborough (1993). This (primary) headteacher explains:

> My definition is that you treat everybody according to their dignity that every human being has irrespective of whether they are children or adults. And you do not measure contributions, verbal or otherwise, according to the status of the person who is making them. That you value everybody's contribution, be it child, be it dinner lady, be it teacher. The children are regularly told that they have to respect the headteacher and that they will be respected by everybody as well. There is this mutual respect notion because we are all human beings. (Headteacher in study by Riseborough 1993: 160)

Human status demands inclusion in opportunities for democratic leadership. This is the implication of developmental democracy. But there are a number of factors which legitimately should be taken into account in considering the degree to which all possible stakeholders are to be included in democratic processes. Delicate balances need to be struck.

Firstly, there are questions to do with boundaries of participation and the degree of participation (the amount of influence which should be exercised democratically by different groups and individuals). The case for involvement of all stakeholders in democratic decision making depends on

- *variability of interests*: Are the interests of all stakeholders in the issues for decision deemed to be equal?

- *variability of capability*: Are the groups with an interest capable of participating and representing their interests?

- *variability of democratic commitment*: Are the groups with interest and capability committed to democratic values and might there be a danger of their subverting the democratic process?

All of these factors involve difficult judgements which themselves deserve democratic scrutiny. Who is to make these judgements is a question in itself. It is essential that groups are not excluded for other reasons, such as the unconscious result of invisible power. Perceptions of variability of capability and democratic commitment in particular raise questions about the distribution of internal authority – who is counted as legitimate and capable of engaging in ethical rationality. It has already been noted that expertise on values and their implications for action according to the contingencies of particular circumstances is not the preserve of positional leaders. In addition, judgements about such issues do not provide once-and-for-all answers. Participation in democratic processes may build up capabilities and commitments to democracy which are initially weak. Indeed, this is exactly a key purpose of developmental democracy, so that, for example, the sensitivities and skills involved in communicative virtues and other capabilities are enhanced through practice. The implication is that some degree of participation should be extended to the youngest students so that these virtues are allowed to develop, though its scope and influence will be appropriately greater for older students.

Secondly, there is the scope of participation, that is the question of what should be open to democratic decision and influence. Gastil's (1997) decision tree for democracy and democratic leadership highlights some of the relevant factors, which are incorporated in the list below. The case for democratic decision making might be viewed as less compelling where an issue is

- *purely technical*: this would be where the nature of the issue or problem is clear and has a 'straightforward technical solution' (p. 166).

- *subject to superior legitimate authority*: an issue or area of activity may be a matter of implementing directions from a higher level in a formal hierarchy of authority, such as national government which draws its ultimate legitimacy from elected representatives in a democratic society.[7]

Often limits within an organisation like a school will be set by overarching organisational values and goals. In education these have been increasingly set by central regulation, performance targets and inter-institutional comparisons aimed at producing skills and attitudes required for the competitive and globally-orientated market economy. Nevertheless, *how* external directions are implemented is likely to be a very important question which should be based on democratic involvement at the point of implementation.

● *subject to cultural determination*: this is less about formal direction than the pressures, assumptions and messages that emanate from groups and cultures which form the context for schooling. For example, certain issues may be taken to be off-limits for democratic debate.

● *a matter of indifference*: this is where the issue or area of activity does not matter to stakeholders. However, it could be that they would not be indifferent if they were fully informed.

● *urgent*: where rapid action is demanded by circumstances, drawn out democratic involvement is often impractical, though post hoc review of decisions is feasible.

It is evident that drawing appropriate boundaries is not a clear-cut matter. Continual alertness is required to the possibility of groups or decisions being excluded from democratic deliberation for reasons that arise from other considerations: self-interest, time restraints, and so on. The challenges of striking the right balance, together with the time, energy and resources involved in democratic rationalities, can lead to an emphasis on formalism. For example, the problem of boundaries can be resolved, on the surface at least, by having representatives of specified stakeholder groups at meetings that only formally and briefly consider a wide range of matters and decisions, giving the process apparent democratic legitimacy. Approached in this way, the best that might be hoped for is a liberal minimalist democratic model in which leaders of interest groups protect their corner.

Avoiding this involves, in part, keeping the leadership eye on the educational ball. Democratic leadership in the developmental model is embedded in people's inherent potential for learning. This vision of learning is not one that is subservient to the measure of learners in a competitive struggle committed to determining the positional status of students. Nor is it consistent with the reduction of democracy to a continual conflict of interests between individuals or between groups within the school community. Day-to-day engagement involves aspiring to put into practice dispersed democratic pedagogies that suffuse the school as a learning community. It involves attempting to explore the principles and rationalities of developmental democracy and the open approach to knowledge through 'creative and risky performances in action' (Joas 2000: 170), forging them together with different emphases and compromises according to circumstances and possibilities.

Finding resources, especially time, is a major practical issue in enabling dispersed democratic leadership. In part, this can be addressed by the development of clear meeting guidelines and delegation of decisions to individuals and groups (Court 2003: 165). There are no easy solutions. Rather, there is a continual need to recognise that, if democratic principles and practices are valued highly and authentic democracy is being sincerely sought, the time for dispersed democratic leadership structured into the organisation should not be silently and insidiously squeezed by other demands. Apple and Bean acknowledge the effort and hard work that democratic education involves by everyone – teachers, administrators and students. But, they go on, the educators engaged in this 'have decided to devote their lives as educators to engaging in educational activity organized around democratic social and pedagogic principles in which they strongly believe. In other words they have chosen to be exhausted as a result of something worthwhile'. (Apple and Bean 1999: 121)

Conclusions: characteristics of practical engagement

Key implications for the exercise of democratic leadership were summarised at the beginning of the chapter, gleaned from earlier chapters which explained and elaborated the developmental conception of democracy. The further discussion of engagement in this chapter has generated additional themes that have something to say about the challenges to practice identified earlier (see Chapter 7): inauthenticity, ineffectiveness, misbalances, minimalism and resources. Practical engagement in democratic leadership makes a number of demands which are important in addressing these issues (though no claim is made that these challenges are thereby resolved):

- profound participation, in the sense of authentic involvement guided by deeply embedded navigational feelings and shared symbols of democratic ideas and ideals;

- a continuing role for lead agency which is both facilitative and plays a decisive part in setting possibilities and guiding principles;

- conscious participation in microgenesis (change through small, creative actions which, if repeated and replicated, create new structural patterns);

● daily actions that create a culture of gifts rather than a culture of injury;

● opening boundaries of participation and consciously striking balances between inclusion based on human status and inclusion based on a complex set of practical considerations and factors;

● keeping the leadership eye on the educational ball and putting into practice dispersed democratic pedagogies that suffuse the school as a learning community;

● committing the time and resources needed to allow the democratic rationalities to be pursued, because they are perceived as educationally valuable.

Characteristics of practical engagement in creating and sustaining democratic leadership, based on the implications highlighted in this chapter, are summarised in Figure 10.1.

- practice of democratic rationalities
- encouraging benign creativity and appreciation of navigational feelings
- valuing autonomy and creative space as necessary for human creativity and flourishing
- encouraging a critical humanism which values each person's humanistic potential and promotes awareness and understanding of the 'hard' realities of modernity
- encouraging an open approach to knowledge
- profound participation (authentic involvement guided by navigational feelings and shared symbols of democratic ideas and ideals)
- lead agency which is facilitative and sets possibilities and guiding principles
- conscious participation in microgenesis
- daily actions that create a culture of gifts rather than a culture of injury
- striking balances concerning the participation of groups according to a complex set of considerations and factors
- keeping the leadership eye on the educational ball and putting into practice dispersed democratic pedagogies throughout the school community
- committing time and resources for democratic rationalities because they are perceived as educationally valuable

---

Figure 10.1: Creating and sustaining democratic leadership – key elements of practical engagement

Notes

1   This summary of implications is derived from the leadership activities alluded to in the discussion of models of democracy (Table 1.1, Chapter 1) and the arguments in Chapters 4 and 5.

2   The idea of ideals as symbols is discussed in more detail in P.A. Woods (2003). In short, the view put forward there is that human action is enabled by symbols (be they tools, roles, ideas, etc.) which have meaning (reflecting the Vygotskian basis of the notion of microgenesis). Amongst these symbols are ideals and notions of self-transcendence (exogenous identity orientations) that are not solely the product of society but point to enduring, super-cultural truths of goodness and value.

3   See Table 7.1, Chapter 7.

4   See Chapter 6.

5   The headteacher was one of a group of headteachers interviewed in 1997 and 1998 as part of the UK, ESRC-funded, Impact of Competition on Secondary Schools (ICOSS) Study. Further details are in Woods (2000) where this headteacher is reported as Head H.

6   The student was one of a group of Year 10 students interviewed in 1998 as part of the ICOSS Study (see note 5). Further details are in Woods and Levačić (2002).

7   A different sort of legitimacy that might be accepted as determining a course of action is that based on expertise and/or capacity for judgement – for example expert advice on health and safety matters. Nevertheless, responsibility for accepting that advice may still properly be a matter for a democratic forum.

11 *Dualities of democratic leadership*

Putting into operation and dispersing a form of democratic leadership based on the developmental model of democracy is ambitious and challenging. Democratic leadership in this broad sense directs educational activity towards the deepest questions and purposes of creative human potential. The breadth of its concern with democratic rationalities and social justice is encapsulated in the principal aims of such leadership, summarised in Figure 11.1.

To create an environment in which people:
- are encouraged and supported in aspiring to truths about the world, including the highest values (ethical rationality)
- practice this ethical rationality and look for ways of superseding difference through dialogue (discursive rationality)
- are active contributors to the creation of the institutions, culture and relationships they inhabit (decisional rationality)
- are empowered and enabled by the institutional, cultural and social structures of the organisation (therapeutic rationality)
- promote respect for diversity and reduce cultural and material inequalities (social justice)

Figure 11.1: Principal aims of democratic leadership

By the very nature of schools and the practical complexity of translating into reality the principles and rationalities of developmental democracy, with all the challenges and obstacles entailed, there is no one model of democratic leadership and schooling which can be advocated. A sense of how, in one instance, it may look in practice is given by a school studied in depth by Jeffrey and Woods (2003) over several years. This is a state primary school in the UK internationally recognised for its imaginative use of the school environment. The affective domain amongst students and staff is encouraged and valued, and is a vibrant part of the whole school life. The

131

following is part of my own description and reflections on the report of their study. Page numbers refer to Jeffrey and Woods (2003).

> Confidence, imagination, enjoyment, humour, the excitement of practical discovery – in other words, emotional senses orientated to positive ends – are integral to the curriculum and stimulated by the school environment. This is in addition to (complementary) analytical and self-organising capabilities which form part of developing the 'children's critical capacities' (p. 89), by peer evaluation amongst other means, and the school's success in national curriculum tests.

> > Feeling positively about learning combines the emotions and the cognitive in an experience that draws the learner inside the activity ... It is of great importance to [the school's] teachers how children feel about their learning. Feelings hold the key to cognition. So there is much talk of excitement, joy, fun, happiness, confidence. (p. 205)

> One of the main sources of the school's success is the 'democratic and collaborative way' (p. 123) it is run, with teachers working 'as a team in which they are all leaders' (p. 126). Accounts from staff and others emphasise the presence of a non-threatening role ambiguity which blurs usual divisions and hierarchical relations amongst staff, students, parents and the community. This provides one example of how a more loosely structured creative space may appear in practice. It is possible to see in the account of the school's leadership signs of the reintegration of human capacities, mirroring the approach to children's learning. Staff are empowered by internal motivations and desires 'to be something special for someone else',[1] and it is clear that the emotional senses which inspire and steer action are celebrated and enhanced in the school. Also apparent is utilisation of organisational and analytical capabilities, which are integral to making navigational feelings count in practice. Such capabilities are evident in the systematic 'strategic redefinition' of the national curriculum, which involved staff in both identifying what was welcome in the latter and adapting it to the school's values (p. 56), and in the headteacher's 'entrepreneurial skills' (p. 125) used to secure funds and services to support ambitious school activities. (Woods 2004: 21)

Even though no one model can be advocated, it is clear nevertheless that in all educational institutions progress towards dispersed democratic leadership requires advances in three areas which constitute the trialectic dynamic of any social order:

- structure;

- people;

- practical engagement.

The principal issues and characteristics for attention and action in relation to each of these areas have been elaborated and summarised in Chapters 8, 9 and 10. Structurally, there is a need for a kind of bivalent architecture which enshrines free space in a democratic frame and which has an institutional dimension (providing specific entitlements, roles and forums that encourage power sharing), a cultural dimension (a shared vision of democratic aims and practice) and a social dimension (the texture of day-to-day relations). With regard to people, there is an array of key capabilities and skills integral to their development as contributors to democratic leadership. With regard to practical engagement in democratic leadership, there is a complex set of interacting and testing actions and strategies.

These set out an ambitious set of ideal aspirations. Ideals, however, become tarnished as soon as they are exposed to reality: 'as the mind turns from the wonderful cloudland of aspiration to the ugly scaffold of attempt and achievement, a succession of opposite ideas arise … '.[2] However rich the conception of democracy is underpinning democratic leadership, lofty ideals cannot be allowed to avert the eyes from studied recognition of the complexity, built-in tensions and flaws within their human expression and social practice. There is no easy or assured path which overcomes human fallibilities and the misuses of visible and invisible power. This is apparent from the obstacles and challenges to democratic leadership discussed in some detail in Chapter 7.

Indeed, at the root of the bivalent character of democracy is a paradox which runs through the practical manifestation of democratic leadership. This bivalence represents the incorporation in democratic arrangements of a dynamic to-and-fro movement between relatively loose and relatively tight structural frameworks – between free space and firm framing. The paradox is the co-existence of openness and fixity which goes with this. On the one hand, the world is turned upside down by a democratic social order, in the sense that values and knowledge are seen as capable of being addressed, understood, questioned and identified by any and all – underpinned by a recognition that there is an individual and shared capacity to generate ethical and meaningful knowledge. This is the destabilising message (destabilising, that is, for conventional hierarchical order) of the religious revolution with which this book opened. The a-religious notion of humanistic potential – more appropriate to the later, contemporary stages of the long march of this revolutionary process – is no less destabilising for conventional hierarchies. It implies the liberty which involves no structure, no status distinctions, no pre-formed ideas or verities, no restrictions.

On the other hand, it is in the nature of democratic orders also to turn the world back from such anti-structural liberty. Certain matters become accepted as known, fixed and taken to have veridical force, and these grow to be part of the background institutional and cultural structure. Their epistemological grounding appears to be more rationalist than critical. And it has to be so. For example, democratic principles of freedom and equal participation and particular institutional arrangements for democratic relations and governance come to have legitimacy and become part of the firm framing in which people live. A school needs to have these translated into organisational arrangements – comprising governing bodies, committees, teams, student councils, chairs, representatives, delegates, facilitators, procedural norms and so on – which participants can utilise and which strengthen the capacity to engage in dispersed leadership. It is the creation of durable roles, forums for debate and decision making, and agreed values, priorities and practices which give opportunities for effectual democratic leadership. Equally, democratic pedagogies take place within a structured framework of roles, understandings and patterns of relationship. Enshrined within these are degrees of equality and status differences (between students and staff, between non-teaching staff, classroom teachers and senior school managers), ideas of educational aims and values, and norms of behaviour.

All of these institutional, cultural and social structures may continue in tandem with democratic leadership and, as previously acknowledged, are a necessary element. But three points need to be emphasised with regard to the paradox. The first is the importance of self-awareness amongst participants that these structures are social creations; the product of negotiations and decisions within the school or, perhaps, in democratic arenas (parliaments, local councils) outside the school. They should be consciously recognised and legitimated. Otherwise status differences, the culture of education, ways of working and norms of behaviour will be expressions of arbitrary power.

Secondly, there is a key question that continually needs to be addressed and returned to concerning any particular democratic structural framework. To what extent is it in practice conducive to dispersed democratic leadership? The paradox in which the bivalent character of democracy is rooted gives rise to structures that are capable of being both used and abused. Old or new statuses, power differences and means of preserving and advancing vested interests may easily be smuggled in. Democracy is political. That is, it is a social order that recognises that there are genuine disagreements about values and priorities and conflicting interests within organisations, and that all of these need to be allowed to contend and engage with each other in agreed processes of decision making. The higher aims of developmental democracy are assailed by the succeeding conflicts and plays of micro-politics. Despite a democratic ethos, teachers, for example, may still have recourse to their professional status in relation to students as a line of defence (Trafford 2003). Equally, the power and institutional authority of the headteacher role does not abate *vis-á-vis* teachers simply because the school is declared to be democratic and collegial. Amongst students there are differences and conflicts which may undermine the goal of fair participation for all. Eternal vigilance, through critical self-evaluation of the organisation, is the price of genuine dispersal of democratic leadership.

Thirdly, the perpetual tension and danger of the arbitrary power which is inherent in the bivalent character of democracy necessitate a perpetual search for balance between holding to what is fixed and giving scope to the challenging and questioning dynamics of free space.

> Wisdom is always to find the appropriate relationship between structure and communitas under the *given* circumstances of time and place, to accept each modality when it is paramount without rejecting the other, and not to cling to one when its present impetus is spent. (Turner 1969:139, original emphasis)

The pervasiveness of this perpetual search for balance is apparent from the number of dualities that can be identified and are associated with the duality of fixity and openness and the bivalent character of democracy. These dualities have emerged during the discussion of the nature of democracy and democratic leadership in prior chapters and, in their different ways, point to the importance of recognising and balancing constraint and unfettered liberty (see Figure 11.2). They include:

- substantive and protective principles, which need to be balanced against each other – substantive principles emphasise belonging in a unifying institution or community (unity) and the importance of some kind of specific view of human potentiality and what it means to be a good person in a good society (substantive liberty), while protective principles emphasise respect for diversity and rights to exercise freedom (see Chapter 1);

- equality and freedom, which in practice need to be weighed against each other in terms of their practical consequences since complete autonomy may have disadvantages for some as against others, as in the operation of democratic pedagogies for example (see Chapter 6);

- rational capacities (manifest in the dominance of instrumental rationality) and affective capacities, and the need to strive for a better balance between these (see Chapter 4);

- the dialectical relationship between rational and critical epistemologies (see Chapter 5);

- firm framing and free space, both of which are integral to a structure conducive to democratic leadership (see Chapter 8);

- lead agency and bottom-up initiative, which each have a place in creating and sustaining democratic leadership (see Chapter 10).

Democratic leadership infuses the life of the school as an educational community. The link between democratic leadership and learning, discussed at length in Chapter 6, is worth reiterating. Democratic leadership, where it is not confined to occasional exercises in participation and involvement, is associated with active, participative learning and democratic pedagogies. Nor is this sort of participative learning limited to students. In a democratic order in which ethical rationality is prime, all learning embraces the genesis of veridical meaning and its critical testing through action and deliberation, so developing the capacities that make ethical rationality possible. All are seekers of greater understanding – truth, if you like – in this kind of active democracy.

Indeed, the conception of what constitutes valued learning is challenged by democratic leadership founded in a developmental understanding of democracy. If students, and staff, are not to be conceived and developed principally as instruments to economic advancement, a fundamental concern is the experience of education. Appreciation of emotional senses and navigational feelings, and the balancing of these with a complementary analytical rationality, rather than a dominant instrumental rationality, are nurtured by the right kind of democratic pedagogies in educational settings. Democratic leadership creates a particular texture of relationships which is supportive of all members of the school community as creative agents with inherent potential. The human development stimulated by this – a sense of mutual identity and support, feelings of empowerment, social and interpersonal capabilities – is itself learning, though not necessarily with outcomes capable of being measured. The learning is that involved in becoming a democratic citizen – a person, both in oneself and with others, capable of profound participation.

Because of the profound involvement of the person, enormous care must be taken with developmental democracy as a philosophy. It is capable of being 'misdeveloped' into a vehicle for oppression of individuals. A 'dark' side of democracy and the dangers of groupthink have been acknowledged (in Chapters 1 and 8 respectively). A critique of developmental democracy might contend

- that it places too much emphasis on the substantive and an over thick conception of the good, at the expense of the procedural;

* that it fails to recognise and understand the ethical diversity which characterises contemporary society.3

In response to these arguments, five points need to be emphasised. Firstly, there is no easy opt-out from deciding between a narrow or broad conception of democracy. The former implies limited individuality, such as the self-interested citizen of liberal minimalism, and, if our educational aim is to support people to become more than this, some broader conception like the developmental model is necessary. Secondly, as has been stressed throughout, all of the democratic rationalities are essential. They are interacting and mutually supportive. Discursive rationality, which endeavours to respect and explore difference, is integral to the processes of democracy, and becomes of even greater importance in societies which are ethically and culturally diverse. Thirdly, a symbiotic relationship with cultural justice, concerned with respect for cultural diversity, is embraced by the developmental model of democracy. Fourthly, an open approach to knowledge characterises the epistemological basis to developmental democracy. Nothing is beyond debate and questioning at some point, including the meaning and interpretation of the good and of key ideas such as humanistic potential. In other words, there is an in-built epistemological safeguard to the oppression of hegemonic ideas. Fifthly, the democratic principles – freedom, equality, organic belonging and substantive liberty – are explicit and it is recognised that they need to be weighed and balanced against each other. Recognition of tensions between them is built into the developmental model, and it is inevitable that such tensions have to be addressed and as far as possible resolved through practical action.

In conclusion, what is it that is most important about democratic leadership? Where it is searched or struggled for, there is an energy behind democratisation that has much in common with the many religious, philosophical and political worldviews that people have created and thronged to over the centuries. This energy manifests itself in two ways. The first is the desire to consciously recognise, counter, challenge and overcome human weaknesses, both individually and as they manifest themselves in social injustices. Democratic ideals are based on an awareness and understanding of human fallibilities, particularly the capacity to abuse power in subtle and not-so-subtle ways in social relationships. The second is in the striving to understand where a source of strength may be found to enable these weaknesses to be overcome and to provide (in religious terminology) salvation. Developmental democracy appreciates the strength of human creativity and growth in each person and the human potential for working together towards higher ends and overcoming disagreement and diversity of interests, without violence. If the term 'salvation' is not used in relation to democracy, there is still some sense of aspiration to an elevated life in company with others that is good for the person and good for society. Accordingly, the point of democratic leadership, grounded in the conception of developmental democracy, is only partially to enable equal participation by all in the decisions that affect them. The primary point is to strive towards a way of living – in and through relationships – which is orientated towards the values that ultimately represent human progress and goodness.

An appeal only to such idealism is insufficient in itself, however. School leaders have to recognise and cope with the mundane pressures of organisational survival within educational policies that place great emphasis on measurable performance. And they also have to be responsive to the practical need for students to gain qualifications and show demonstrable achievement in skills that will help them find employment in the wider society. It is appropriate, therefore, to test democratic leadership and democratic pedagogies according to the degree to which they contribute to attainment in these kinds of measurable and instrumental outcomes. Research suggests that the relationship between democratic leadership and measurable outcome is not a simple one. There is, nevertheless, sufficient evidence about the significance for learning of democratic principles and practices, such as participation, engagement and empowerment, to commend democratic leadership as a resource for organisational success in the narrower sense defined by a performative culture (see Chapter 6). In other words, there are good reasons for cultivating democratic leadership in pursuit of this kind of success.

In practice, the advancement of democratic leadership, as with social action more generally, is likely to proceed through a mixture of motivations, with ideals *and* a concern for organisational interests intermingling. Indeed, another of the dualities of democratic leadership – the positive enabling of creative potential together with a recognition of the 'hard' realities of modernity – was recognised in Chapter 4. This duality between the open potential of creativity and the constraints of an over-rationalising, alienating and economistic social order characterised by diverse structural inequalities, constitutes the background for the intrinsic and instrumental arguments for democratic leadership. There are tensions in balancing this duality, as there are with the other dualities that have been highlighted (see Figure 11.2). However, a combination of intrinsic and instrumental arguments forms a powerful incentive for developing and dispersing democratic leadership.

It remains vital, nevertheless, not to lose the idealistic aspirations bound up with democratic leadership. Developmental democracy stems from a particular understanding of humanistic potential. This is why ethical rationality is 'first among equals' amongst the four democratic rationalities. At the same time, the orientation of democratic leadership is social. It concerns the social and cultural order in which people live together. It is the outward manifestation of inner potential, and all of the democratic rationalities are needed to constitute a full democratic order. The purpose of democratic leadership is to create and help sustain an environment that enables everyone belonging to it who is deemed a free, creative agent to be part of these interlinking democratic rationalities. Hence it has an intimate relationship with social justice. A concern to realise democratic participation springs from not only a sense of humanistic potential, but also recognition of the material significance of distributive injustices.[4] The aims of democratic leadership (see Figure 11.1) derive from these fundamental impulses. In short, democratic leadership is concerned with enabling people to *share power* (by dispersing leadership and diminishing hierarchy), *share hope* (by extending opportunities to realise humanistic potential) and *share the fruits of society* (through fair distribution of resources and cultural respect).

Fixity	Openness
• substantive principles (unity, substantive liberty)	• protective principles (diversity, freedom)
• equality	• freedom
• rational capacities	• affective capacities
• rational epistemology	• critical epistemology
• firm framing	• free space
• lead agency	• 'bottom-up' initiative
• 'hard' realities of modernity	• creative potential

Figure 11.2: Dualities of democratic leadership

Notes

1   Heath (1993: 266), quoted by Jeffrey and Woods (2003: 133) in their analysis of the school's culture.
2   Winston Churchill, quoted in Ferguson (2003: xxv).
3   Olssen et al. (2004) articulate concerns about Macpherson's thesis on liberalism (which challenges possessive individualism) – namely that it is perfectionist, too utopian, emphasises the substantive over the procedural, has an over thick conception of the good, and 'fails to appreciate the extent to which we live in a pluralistic world of ethical diversity' (p. 95). These could be raised about developmental democracy. I have taken the essential points and expressed them in the two challenges articulated in the main text.
4   See Figure 2.2, Chapter 2.

Bibliography

Airey, J., Drewett-Gray, J. and Flecknoe, M. (2004) 'Pupil agency in directing learning: a crossover trial'. Paper presented at 7th International BELMAS/SCRELM Research Conference, St Catherine's College, Oxford, 8–10 July.

Annette, J. (2003) 'Community, politics and citizenship education', in A. Lockyer, B. Crick and J. Annette (eds), *Education for Democratic Citizenship*. Aldershot: Ashgate.

Apple, M.W. (2000) *Official Knowledge: Democratic Education in a Conservative Age*. New York: Routledge.

Apple, M.W. and Bean, J.A. (1999) 'Lessons from democratic schools', in M.W. Apple and J.A. Bean (eds), *Democratic Schools: Lessons from the Chalk Face*. Buckingham: Open University Press.

Archer, M. (1995) *Realist Social Theory: The Morphogenetic Approach*. Cambridge: Cambridge University Press.

Archer, M. (2003) *Being Human: The Problem of Agency*. Cambridge: Cambridge University Press.

Arnot, M. and Reay, D. (2003) 'The framing of pedagogic encounters: regulating the social order in classroom learning'. Paper presented to British Educational Research Association Conference, Heriot-Watt University, Edinburgh 11–13 September.

Ashley, M. with Barnes, S. (1999) 'Citizenship: a new word for humanities', in M. Ashley (ed.), *Improving Teaching and Learning in the Humanities*. London: Falmer, pp. 139–61.

Ball, S.J. (1987) *The Micro-Politics of the School*. London: Methuen.

Ball, S.J. (2000) 'Performativities and fabrications in the education economy: towards the performative society', *Australian Educational Researcher*, 27 (2): 1–24.

Barbalet, J.M. (2001) *Emotion, Social Theory, and Social Structure*. Cambridge: Cambridge University Press.

Benjamin, B. (1992) *An Aristocracy of Everyone*. Oxford: Oxford University Press.

Bennett, N. and Anderson, L. (2003) 'Introduction: rethinking educational leadership – challenging the conventions', in N. Bennett and L. Anderson (eds), *Rethinking Educational Leadership*. London: Sage.

Bennett, N., Harvey, J.A., Wise, C. and Woods, P.A. (2003a) *Desk Study Review of*

Distributed Leadership. Nottingham: NCSL/CEPAM. Available at: http://www.ncsl.org.uk/literaturereviews.

Bennett, N., Wise, C., Woods, P.A. and Newton, W. (2003b) 'Leading from the middle: a review and analysis of the evidence'. Paper presented to British Educational Research Association Conference, Heriot-Watt University, Edinburgh, 11–13 September.

Berger, P. (1973) *A Rumour of Angels*. Harmondsworth: Penguin Books.

Bernstein, B. (1996) *Pedagogy, Symbolic Control and Identity*. London: Taylor & Francis.

Bickmore, K. (2001) 'Student conflict resolution, power "sharing" in schools, and citizenship education', *Curriculum Inquiry*, 31 (2): 137–62.

Blackmore, J. (1990) 'School-based decision-making and teacher unions: the appropriation of a discourse', in J. Chapman (ed), *School-based Decision-making and Management*. London: Falmer.

Blackmore, J. (1999) *Troubling Women*. Buckingham: Open University Press.

Blair, M. (2001) *Why Pick On Me? School Exclusion and Black Youth*. Stoke-on-Trent: Trentham.

Blase, J. and Blase, J. (1999) 'Implementation of shared governance for instructional improvement: principals' perspectives', *Journal of Educational Administration*, 37 (5): 476–500.

Blatchford, P. (1998) *Social Life in School: Pupils' Experience of Breaktime and Recess from 7 to 16 years*. London: Falmer.

Bottery, M. (1992) *The Ethics of Educational Management*. London: Cassell.

Bottery, M. (2001) 'Globalisation and the UK competition state: no room for transformational leadership in education?', *School Leadership & Management*, 21 (2): 199–218.

Bottery, M. (2002) 'Educational leadership and economic realities', *Educational Management Administration and Leadership*, 30 (2): 157–74.

Bottery, M. (2003) 'The management and mismanagement of trust', *Educational Management and Administration*, 31 (3): 245–61.

Bottery, M. (2004) 'Education and globalisation: redefining the role of the educational professional'. Inaugural lecture, University of Hull, Hull, 15 March.

Boucher, D. and Vincent, A. (2000) *British Idealism and Political Theory*. Edinburgh: Edinburgh University Press.

Burbules, N. (1993) *Dialogue in Teaching: Theory and Practice*. New York: Teachers College Press.

Burns, J.M. (1978) *Leadership*. New York: Harper and Row.

Bush, T. and Glover, D. (2003) *School Leadership: Concepts and Evidence*. Nottingham: National College of School Leadership.

Bush, T. and Heysteck, J. (2003) 'School governance in the new South Africa'. *Compare*, 33 (2): 127–38.

Campbell, C., Gold, A. and Lunt, I. (2003) 'Articulating leadership values in action: conversations with school leaders', *International Journal of Leadership in Education*, 6 (3): 203–22.

Carr, D. (2000) *Professionalism and Ethics in Teaching*. London: Routledge.

Carr, W. and Hartnett, A. (1996) *Education and the Struggle for Democracy*. Buckingham: Open University Press.

Chandler, D. (2001) 'Active citizens and the therapeutic state: the role of democratic participation in local government reform', *Policy and Politics*, 29 (1): 3–14.

Cheng, K. (2004) 'Learning in a knowledge society: the democratic dimension', in J. MacBeath and L. Moos (eds), *Democratic Learning: The Challenge to School Effectiveness*. London: RoutledgeFalmer.

Cheung, F. and Cheng, Y. C. (2002) 'An outlier study of multilevel self-management and school performance', *School Effectiveness and School Improvement*, 13 (3): 253–90.

Ciulla, J.B. (1998) 'Leadership and the problem of bogus empowerment', in J.B. Ciulla (ed.), *Ethics: The Heart of Leadership*. Westport, CT: Praeger.

Clegg, S.R. (1989) *Frameworks of Power*. London: Sage.

Clough, N. and Holden, C. (2002) *Education for Citizenship: Ideas into Action – A Practical Guide for Teachers of Pupils aged 7–14*. London: Routledge/Falmer.

Cooper, B. (2003) 'Teachers who care in a system that does not: the moral failure of the education system'. Paper presented at British Educational Research Association Conference, Heriot-Watt University, Edinburgh, 11–13 September.

Court, M. (2003) 'Towards democratic leadership: co-principal initiatives', *International Journal of Leadership in Education*, 6 (2): 161–83.

Court, M. (2004) 'Talking back to new public management versions of accountability in education: a co-principalship's practices of mutual responsibility', *Educational Management Administration and Leadership*, 32 (2): 171–94.

Cribb, A. and Gewirtz, S. (2003) 'Towards a sociology of just practices: an analysis of plural conceptions of justice', in C. Vincent (ed.), *Social Justice, Education and Identity*. London: RoutledgeFalmer.

Croninger, R.G. and Malen, B. (2002) 'The role of school governance in the creation of school community', in K. Leithwood, P. Hallinger, K. Seashore-Louis, G. Furman-Brown, P. Gronn, W. Mulford and K. Riley (eds), *Second International Handbook of Educational Leadership and Administration*. Dordrecht: Kluwer.

Cunningham, J. (2000) 'Democratic practice in a secondary school', in A. Osler (ed.), *Citizenship and Democracy in Schools: Diversity, Identity, Equality*. Stoke-on-Trent: Trentham Books. pp. 133–41.

Day, C. and Harris, A. (2003) 'Teacher leadership, reflective practice and school improvement', in *International Handbook of Educational Administration*. Dordrecht: Kluwer. pp. 724–49.

Day, C., Harris, A., Hadfield, M., Tolley, H. and Beresford, J. (2000) *Leading Schools in Times of Change*. Buckingham: Open University Press.

Deem, R., Brehony, K. and Heath, S. (1995) *Active Citizenship and the Governing of Schools*. Buckingham: Open University Press.

Den Otter, S.M. (1996) *British Idealism and Social Explanation*. Oxford: Clarendon Press.

Donaldson, M. (1993) *Human Minds*. London: Penguin.

Earley, P. and Evans, J. (2004) 'Making a difference? Leadership development for headteachers and deputies – ascertaining the impact of the National College for School Leadership', *Educational Management, Administration and Leadership*, 32 (3): 325–38.

Engestrom, Y. (1999) 'Activity theory and individual and social transformation', in Y. Engestrom, R. Miettinen and R-L. Punamaki (eds), *Perspectives on Activity Theory*. Cambridge: Cambridge University Press.

Engestrom, Y. (2000) 'Comment on Blackler et al. Activity theory and the social construction of knowledge: a story of four umpires', *Organization*, 7 (2): 301–10.

Ferguson, N. (2003) *Empire: How Britain made the Modern World*. London: Penguin.

Fevre, R.W. (2000) *The Demoralization of Western Culture*. London: Continuum.

Fielding, M. (1999) 'Radical collegiality: affirming teaching as an inclusive professional practice', *Australian Educational Researcher*, 26 (2): 1–34.

Fielding, M. (2001) 'OFSTED, inspection and the betrayal of democracy', *Journal of Philosophy of Education*, 35 (4): 695–709.

Fielding, M. (2004) 'Transformative approaches to student voice: theoretical underpinnings, recalcitrant realities', *British Educational Research Journal*, 30 (2): 295–311.

Flecknoe, M. (2004) 'Challenging the orthodoxies: putting a spoke into the vicious cycle', *Educational Management, Administration and Leadership*, 32 (4): 405–22.

Fraser, N. (1997) *Justice Interruptus: Critical Reflections on the 'Postsocialist' Condition*. London: Routledge.

Freire, P. (1985) *The Politics of Education*. Granby, MA: Bergin and Garvey.

Fromm, E. (1961) *Marx's Concept of Man*. New York: Frederick Ungar Publishing.

Fullan, M. (2001) *Leading in a Culture of Change*. San Francisco: Jossey-Bass.

Fullan, M. (2003) *The Moral Imperative of School Leadership*. Thousand Oaks, CA: Corwin Press.

Furman, G. (ed.) (2002) *School as Community*. Albany, NY: State University of New York Press.

Gastil, J. (1997) 'A definition and illustration of democratic leadership', in K. Grint (ed.), *Leadership: Classical, Contemporary and Critical Approaches*. Oxford: Oxford University Press.

Gewirtz, S. (2000) 'Bringing the politics back in: a critical analysis of quality discourses in education', *British Journal of Educational Studies*, 48 (4): 352–70.

Ghandi, M. (1949) *An Autobiography: The Story of my Experiments with Truth*. London: Phoenix Press.

Giddens, A. (1994) *Beyond Left and Right*. Cambridge: Polity Press.

Ginsberg, R. and Davies, T.G. (2003) 'The emotional side of leadership', in N.

Bennett, M. Crawford and M. Cartwright (eds), *Effective Educational Leadership*. London: Paul Chapman.

Giroux, H.A. (1989) *Schooling for Democracy: Critical Pedagogy in the Modern Age*. London: Routledge.

Glatter, R. (2003) 'Collaboration, collaboration, collaboration: the origins and implications of a policy', *Management in Education*, 17 (5): 16–20.

Glatter, R. (2004) 'Leadership and leadership development', in J. Storey (ed.), *Leadership in Organizations: Current Issues and Key Trends*. London: Routledge.

Glickman, C.D. (1998) *Revolutionizing America's Schools*. San Francisco: Jossey-Bass.

Glickman, C.D. (2003) *Holding Sacred Ground: Essays on Leadership, Courage and Endurance in our Schools*. San Francisco: Jossey-Bass.

Gold, A., Evans, J., Earley, P., Halpin, D. and Collarbone, P. (2002) 'Principled principals? Values-driven leadership: evidence from ten case studies of "outstanding school leaders"', *Educational Management and Administration*, 31 (2): 127–38.

Goldstein, J. (2003) 'Making sense of distributed leadership: the case of Peer Assistance Review', *Educational Evaluation and Policy Analysis*, 25 (4): 397–421.

Goodson, I.F. (2003) *Professional Knowledge, Professional Lives*. Maidenhead: Open University Press.

Grace, G. (1995) *School Leadership: Beyond Education Management*, London: Falmer.

Grace, G. (2001) 'Contemporary School Leadership: Reflections on Morrison', *British Journal of Educational Studies*. 49 (4): 386–91.

Graetz, F. (2000) 'Strategic change leadership', *Management Decision*, 38 (8): 550–62.

Gratton, L. (2004) *The Democratic Enterprise*. London: FT/Prentice Hall.

Green, T.H. (1886) 'The sense of "freedom" in morality', in R.L. Nettleship (ed.), *Works of Thomas Hill Green* (Volume II). London: Longmans, Green & Co.

Griffiths, M. (2003) *Action for Social Justice in Education*. Maidenhead: Open University Press.

Grimshaw, D., Vincent, S. and Willmott, H. (2002) 'Going privately: partnership and outsourcing in UK public services', *Public Administration*, 80 (3): 475–502.

Grint, K. (2005) *Leadership: Limits and Possibilities*. Basingstoke: Palgrave Macmillan.

Gronn, P. (1998) 'From transactions to transformation: a new world order in the study of leadership?', in M. Strain, B. Dennison, J. Ousten and V. Hall (eds), *Policy, Leadership and Professional Knowledge in Education*. London: Paul Chapman.

Gronn, P. (1999) 'Substitution for leadership: the neglected role of the leadership couple', *Leadership Quarterly*, 10 (1): 41–62.

Gronn, P. (2000) 'Distributed properties: a new architecture for leadership', *Edu-*

cational Management and Administration, 28 (3): 317–38.

Gronn, P. (2002) 'Distributed leadership', in K. Leithwood, P. Hallinger, K. Seashore-Louis, G. Furman-Brown, P. Gronn, W. Mulford and K. Riley (eds), *Second International Handbook of Educational Leadership and Administration*. Dordrecht: Kluwer.

Gronn, P. and Hamilton, A. (2004) '"A bit more life in the leadership": co-principalship as distributed leadership practice', *Leadership and Policy in Schools*, 3 (1): 3–35.

Gunter, H.M. (2001) *Leaders and Leadership in Education*. London: Paul Chapman.

Habermas, J. (1974) *Theory and Practice*. London: Heinemann.

Hallinger, P. and Heck, R. (1999) 'Can leadership enhance school effectiveness?', in T. Bush, L. Bell, R. Glatter and P. Ribbins (eds), *Educational Management: Redefining Theory, Policy and Practice*, London: Paul Chapman.

Hallinger, P. and Kantamara, P. (2000) 'Educational change in Thailand: opening a window onto leadership as a cultural process', *School Leadership and Management*, 20 (2):189–205.

Harber, C. (1998) 'Education and democracy in Britain and Southern Africa', in C. Harber (ed.), *Voices for Democracy*. Nottingham: Education Now.

Hargreaves, A. (1994) *Changing Teachers, Changing Times: Teachers' Work and Culture in the Postmodern Age*. London: Cassell.

Hargreaves, A. (2003) *Teaching in the Knowledge Society*. Maidenhead: Open University Press.

Hargreaves, A. (2004) 'Distinction and disgust', *International Journal of Leadership in Education*, 7 (1): 27–41.

Hargreaves, D.H. (2003) *Working Laterally: How Innovation Networks make an Education Epidemic*. London: DfES.

Harris, A. (2004) 'Distributed leadership and school improvement: leading or misleading?', *Educational Management, Administration and Leadership*, 32 (1): 11–24.

Harris, A. and Chapman, C. (2002) 'Democratic leadership for school improvement in challenging contexts'. Paper presented to International Congress on School Effectiveness and Improvement, Copenhagen. pp. 23–25. Available at: http://www.ncsl.org.uk.

Hart, S., Dixon, A., Drummond, M.J., and McIntyre, D. (2004) *Learning Without Limits*. Maidenhead: Open University Press.

Hartley, D. (2003) 'The instrumentalisation of the expressive in education', *British Journal of Educational Studies*, 51 (1): 6–19.

Heath, S.B. (1993) 'The madness of reading and writing ethnography', *Anthropology and Education Quarterly*, 24 (3): 251–68.

Held, D. (1996) *Models of Democracy* (Second Edition). Cambridge: Polity Press.

Hellesnes, J. (1976) *Socialisering og Technokrati [Socialisation and Technocracy]*. Copenhagen: Gyldendal.

Henderson, J.G (1999) 'The journey of democratic leadership: an overview', in

J.G. Henderson and K.R. Kesson (eds), *Understanding Democratic Curriculum Leadership*. New York: Teachers College Press.

Hennis, W. (1988) *Max Weber: Essays in Reconstruction*. Hemel Hempstead: Allen & Unwin.

Hill, C. (1940) *The English Revolution 1640*. Published originally by Lawrence and Wishart. Available at: http//www.marxists.org/archive/hill-christopher/english-revolution/.

Hill, C. (1975) *The World Turned Upside Down*. Harmondsworth: Penguin.

Hill, C. (1990) *God's Englishman: Oliver Cromwell and the English Revolution*. London: Penguin.

Hill. C. (1997) *The Intellectual Origins of the English Revolution*. Oxford: Oxford University Press.

Holland, D., Lachicotte, W., Skinner, D. and Cain, C. (1998) *Identity and Agency in Cultural Worlds*. Cambridge, MA, and London: Harvard University Press.

Horner, M. (2003) 'Leadership theory reviewed', in N. Bennett, M. Crawford and M. Cartwright (eds), *Effective Educational Leadership*. London: Paul Chapman.

Hughes, A.C. (1951) *Education and the Democratic Ideal*. London: Longmans, Green and Co.

Hume, D. (1969 [1739/40]) *A Treatise of Human Nature*. Harmondsworth: Penguin.

Inman, S. with Burke, H. (2002) *Schools Councils: An Apprenticeship in Democracy?* London: Association of Lecturers and Teachers.

Jeffrey, B. (2003) 'Countering learner "Instrumentalism" through creative mediation', *British Journal of Educational Research*, 29 (4): 489–503.

Jeffrey, R and Woods, P.E. (2003) *The Creative School*. London: RoutledgeFalmer.

Joas, H. (2000) *The Genesis of Values*. Cambridge: Polity Press.

Jones, K. with Franks, A. (1999) 'English', in D. Hill and M. Cole (eds), *Promoting Equality in Secondary Schools*. London: Cassell.

Jorgensen, P.S. (2004) 'Children's participation in a democratic learning environment', in J. MacBeath and L. Moos (eds), *Democratic Learning: The Challenge to School Effectiveness*. London: RoutledgeFalmer.

Karkkainen, M. (2000) 'Teams as network builders: analysing network contacts in Finnish elementary school teacher teams', *Scandinavian Journal of Educational Research*, 44 (4): 371–91.

Kelly, A.V. (1995) *Education and Democracy: Principles and Practice*. London: Paul Chapman.

Kets de Vries, M.F.R. (1999) 'High-performance teams: lessons from the pygmies', *Organizational Dynamics*, Winter: 66–77.

Keyes, M.W., Hanley-Maxwell, C. and Capper, C.A. (1999) '"Spirituality? It's the core of my leadership": empowering leadership in an inclusive elementary school', *Educational Administration Quarterly*, 35 (2): 203–37.

Klein, R. (2003) *We Want Our Say: Children as Active Participants in their Education*. Stoke-on-Trent: Trentham.

Knight, T. (2001) 'Longitudinal development of educational theory: democracy and the classroom', *Journal of Education Policy*, 16 (3): 249–63.

Kogan, M. (1986) *Education Accountability: An Analytic Overview*. London: Hutchinson.

Lawler, E.E. (2001) 'The era of human capital has finally arrived', in W. Bennis, G.M. Spreitzer and T.G. Cummings (eds), *The Future of Leadership*. San Francisco: Jossey-Bass. pp. 14–25.

Lawrence, E. (1970) *The Origins and Growth of Modern Education*. Harmondsworth: Penguin.

Leithwood, K. and Duke, D.L. (1999) 'A century's quest to understand school leadership', in J. Murphy and K. Seashore Louis (eds), *Handbook of Research on Educational Administration* (Second Edition). San Francisco: Jossey-Bass.

Leithwood, K. and Jantzi, D. (2000) 'Principal and teacher leadership effects: a replication', *School Leadership and Management*, 20 (4): 415–34.

Little, J.W. (2003) 'Constructions of teacher leadership in three periods of policy and reform activism'. Paper presented at Economic and Social Research Council Seminar 'Challenging the Orthodoxy of Leadership', National College for School Leadership, Nottingham, 3 June.

Lingard, B., Hayes, D., Mills, M. and Christie, P. (2003) *Leading Learning*. Maidenhead: Open University Press.

Lockyer, A. (2003) 'The political status of children and young people', in A. Lockyer, B. Crick and J. Annette (eds), *Education for Democratic Citizenship*. Aldershot: Ashgate.

Lowith, K. (1993) *Max Weber and Karl Marx*. London: Routledge.

Lowndes, V. (1999) 'Rebuilding trust in central/local relations: policy or passion?', special issue on *Renewing Local Democracy? The Modernisation Agenda in British Local Government*, in L. Pratchett (ed.), *Local Government Studies*, 25 (4): 116–36.

MacBeath, J. (2004) 'Democratic learning and school effectiveness: are they by any chance related?', in J. MacBeath and L. Moos (eds), *Democratic Learning: The Challenge to School Effectiveness*. London: RoutledgeFalmer.

MacDonald, A. (2004) 'Primary teachers in post-McCrone Scotland', *British Educational Research Journal*, 30 (3): 413–33.

Macpherson, C.B. (1962) *The Political Theory of Possessive Individualism: Hobbes to Locke*. Oxford: Oxford University Press.

Martin, J. (1999) 'Social justice, education policy and the role of parents: a question of choice or voice?', *Education and Social Justice*, 1 (2): 48–61.

Martin, J., Tett, L. and Kay, H. (1999) 'Developing collaborative partnerships: limits and possibilities for schools, parents and community education', *International Studies in Sociology of Education*, 9 (1): 59–75.

Marx, K. (1973) *Grundrisse*. Harmondsworth: Penguin.

Meier, D. and Schwarz, P. (1999) 'Central Park East Secondary School: The hard part is making it happen', in M.W. Apple and J.A. Bean (eds), *Democratic Schools: Lessons from the Chalk Face*. Buckingham: Open University Press.

Meszaros, I. (1970) *Marx's Theory of Alienation*. London: Merlin Press.

Mills, M. (1997) 'Towards a disruptive pedagogy', *International Studies in Sociology of Education*, 7 (1): 35–55.

Mintzberg, H., Simons, R. and Basu, K. (2002) 'Beyond selfishness', *MIT Sloan Management Review*, Fall: 67–74.

Mitchell, C. and Sackney, L. (2000) *Profound Improvement: Building Capacity for a Learning Community*. Netherlands: Swets & Zeitlinger.

Mitchell, H. and Wild, M. (2004) 'Placing the child in childhood', *British Educational Research Journal*, 30 (5): 731–39.

Moos, L. (2004) 'Introduction', in J. MacBeath and L. Moos (eds), *Democratic Learning: The Challenge to School Effectiveness*. London: RoutledgeFalmer.

Muijs, D. and Harris, A. (2003) 'Teacher leadership – improvement through empowerment?', *Educational Management and Administration*, 31 (4): 437–48.

Mulford, B. (2003) 'Balance and learning: crucial elements in leadership for democratic schools', 2 (2): 109–24.

Mulford, B. and Silins, H. (2003) 'Leadership for organisational learning and improved outemes: what do we know?', *Cambridge Journal of Education*, 33 (2): 175–95.

Neill, A.S. (1990) *Summerhill*. London: Penguin.

Nemiroff, G.H. (1992) *Reconstructing Education: Toward a Pedagogy of Critical Humanism*. New York: Bergin & Garvey.

Nettleship, R.L. (1906) 'Memoir', in R.L. Nettleship (ed.), *Works of Thomas Hill Green*, Vol III, *Miscellanies and Memoir*. London: Longmans, Green and Co.

Nixon, J., Martin, J., McKeown, P. and Ranson, S. (1997) 'Towards a learning society: changing codes of occupational practice within the new management of education', *British Journal of Sociology of Education*, 18 (1): 5–28.

Northouse, P.G. (2004) *Leadership: Theory and Practice* (Third Edition), Thousand Oaks, CA: Sage.

Olssen, M., Codd, J. and O'Neill, A-M. (2004) *Education Policy: Globalization, Citizenship and Democracy*. London: Sage.

O'Neill, B. (2002) *Distributive Leadership: Meaning Practice*. Milton Keynes: The Open University.

O'Neill, M., Webster, M. and Woods, P.A. (2003) *New Arrivals: Report of Research on Effective Inclusion of Newly Arrived Families and Pupils to Leicester City Education*. Leicester: Government Office East Midlands and Leicester Education Authority.

Peck, C.A., Gallucci, C., and Staub, D. (2002) 'Children with severe disabilities in regular classrooms: risk and opportunity for creating inclusive communities', in G. Furman (ed.), *School as Community*. Albany, NY: State University of New York Press.

Phillips, A. (2005) 'Participation, inequality, self-interest', in G. Crozier and D. Reay (eds), *Activating Participation*. Stoke-on-Trent: Trentham Books.

Popper, K. (1979) *Objective Knowledge*. Oxford: Clarendon Press.

Power, S and Gewirtz, S. (2001) 'Reading education action zones', *Journal of Education Policy*, 16 (1): 39–51.

Pring, R. (1996) 'Markets, education and Catholic schools', in T. McLaughlin, J. O'Keefe and B. O'Keeffe (eds), *The Contemporary Catholic School*. London: Falmer.

Quicke, J. (2000) 'A new professionalism for a collaborative culture of organizational learning in contemporary society', *Educational Management and Administration*, 28 (3): 299–315.

Ray, T., Clegg, S. and Gordon, R. (2004) 'A new look at dispersed leadership: power, knowledge and context', in J. Storey (ed.), *Leadership in Organizations: Current Issues and Key Trends*. London: Routledge.

Rees, B. (1987) 'Wandering in the wilderness', in J. Robinson and D. Lonsdale (eds), *Can Spirituality Be Taught?* London: Association of Centres of Adult Theological Education and British Council of Churches.

Reitzug, U.C. and O'Hair, M.J. (2002) 'Tensions and struggles in moving toward a democratic school community', in G. Furman (ed.), *School as Community*. Albany, NY: State University of New York Press.

Richmon, M. and Allison, D. (2003) 'Toward a conceptual framework for leadership inquiry', *Educational Management and Administration*, 31 (1): 31–50.

Riley, K. (2004) 'Reforming for democratic schooling: learning for the future not yearning for the past', in J. MacBeath and L. Moos (eds), *Democratic Learning: The Challenge to School Effectiveness*. London: RoutledgeFalmer.

Riseborough, G.F. (1985) 'Pupils, teachers' careers and schooling: an empirical study', in S.J. Ball and I.F. Goodson (eds), *Teachers' Lives and Careers*. Lewes: Falmer.

Riseborough, G.F. (1993) 'Primary headship, state policy and the challenge of the 1990s: an exceptional study that disproves total hegemonic rule', *Journal of Education Policy*, 8 (2): 155–73.

Robertson, J.M. and Webber, C. (2002) 'Boundary-breaking leadership: a must for tomorrow's learning communities', in K. Leithwood, P. Hallinger, K. Seashore-Louis, G. Furman-Brown, P. Gronn, W. Mulford and K. Riley (eds), *Second International Handbook of Educational Leadership and Administration*. Dordrecht: Kluwer.

Rose, P. (2003) 'Community participation in school policy and practice in Malawi: balancing local knowledge, national policies and international agency priorities', *Compare*, 33 (1): 47–64.

Ruddock, J. and Flutter, J. (2004) *How to Improve Your School: Giving Pupils a Voice*. London: Continuum.

Ryan, J. (2002) 'Leadership in contexts of diversity and accountability', in K. Leithwood, P. Hallinger, K. Seashore-Louis, G. Furman-Brown, P. Gronn, W. Mulford and K. Riley (eds), *Second International Handbook of Educational Leadership and Administration*. Dordrecht: Kluwer.

Sachs, J. (2003) *The Activist Teaching Profession*. Buckingham: Open University Press.

Sanderson, I. (1999) 'Participation and democratic renewal: from "instrumental" to "communicative rationality"?', *Policy and Politics*, 27 (3): 325–41.

Saward, M. (2003) *Democracy*. Cambridge: Polity Press.

Schon, D.A. (1991) *The Reflective Practitioner*. Aldershot: Ashgate.

Schroeder, R. (1991) '"Personality" and "inner distance": the conception of the individual in Max Weber's sociology', *History of the Social Sciences*, 4 (1): 325–41.

Sen, A. (1999) 'Democracy as a universal value', *Journal of Democracy*, 10 (3): 3–17.

Sidorkin, A.M. (1999) *Beyond Discourse: Education, the Self and Dialogue*. Albany, NY: State of New York Press.

Simmel, G. (1964) *The Sociology of Georg Simmel*. Edited and translated by K.H. Wolff. New York: The Free Press.

Simmel, G. (1997) 'Spatial and urban culture', in D. Frisby and M. Featherstone (eds), *Simmel on Culture*. London: Sage.

Smith, M. (2002) 'The School Leadership Initiative: an ethically flawed project?', *Journal of Philosophy of Education*, 36 (1): 21–39.

Smyth, J. (2001) 'A culture of teaching "under new management"', in D. Gleeson and C. Husbands (eds), *The Performing School: Managing Teaching and Learning in a Performance Culture*. London: RoutledgeFalmer.

Smyth, J. and Shacklock, G. (1998) *Re-Making Teaching: Ideology, Policy and Practice*. London: Routledge

Spaulding, A. (1997) 'Life in schools – a qualitative study of teacher perspectives on the politics of principals: ineffective leadership behaviours and their consequences upon teacher thinking and behaviour', *School Leadership and Management*, 17 (1): 39–55.

Spillane, J.P., Halverson, R. and Diamond, J.B. (2001) 'Investigating school leadership practice: a distributive perspective', *Educational Researcher*, April: 23–8.

Stokes, G. (2002) 'Democracy and citizenship', in A. Carter and G. Stokes (eds), *Democratic Theory Today*. Cambridge: Polity Press.

Storey, J. (2004) 'Changing theories of leadership and leadership development', Storey (ed.), *Leadership in Organizations: Current Issues and Key Trends*. London: Routledge.

Surowiecki, J. (2004) *The Wisdom of Crowds*. London: Little, Brown.

Suzuki, I. (2002) 'Parental participation and accountability in primary schools in Uganda', *Compare*, 32 (2): 243–59.

Thrupp, M. and Willmott, R. (2003) *Education Management in Managerialist Times*. Maidenhead: Open University Press.

Touraine, A. (1997) *What is Democracy?* Boulder, CO: Westview Press.

Trafford, B. (2003) *School Councils, School Democracy, School Improvement: Why What, How*. Leicester: Secondary Heads Association.

Turner, V.W. (1969) *The Ritual Process: Structure and Anti-Structure*. London: Routledge & Kegan Paul.

Turner, V.W. (1982) *From Ritual to Theatre: The Human Seriousness of Play*. New York: PAJ Publications.

Vincent, C. and Martin, J. (2005) 'Parents as citizens: making the case', in G. Crozier and D. Reay (eds), *Activating Participation*. Stoke-on-Trent: Trentham Books.

von Weltzien Hoivik, H. (2002) 'Accessing, managing and sustaining moral values: a case study', in H. von Weltzien Hoivik (ed.), *Moral Leadership in Action: Building and Sustaining Moral Competence in European Organizations*. Cheltenham: Edward Elgar.

Wallace, M. (1998) 'A counter-policy to subvert education reform? Collaboration among schools and colleges in a competitive climate', *British Educational Research Journal*, 24 (2): 195–215.

Wallace, M. (2003) 'Managing the unmanageable? Coping with complex change', *Educational Management, Administration and Leadership*, 31 (1): 9–29.

Weber, M. (1971) [1930 –translated by Talcott Parsons]) *The Protestant Ethic and the Spirit of Capitalism*. London: Allen & Unwin.

Weber, M. (2001)[1910]) 'Weber's second reply to Rachfahl, 1910', in D. J. Chalcraft and A. Harrington (eds), *The Protestant Ethic Debate: Max Weber's Replies to his Critics, 1907–1910*. Liverpool: Liverpool University Press.

Wells, G.C. (2001) 'Issues of language and translation in Max Weber's protestant ethic writings', *Max Weber Studies*, 2 (1): 33–40.

West-Burnham, J. (2003) 'Education, leadership and the community', in T. Gelsthorpe and J. West-Burnham (eds), *Educational Leadership and the Community: Strategies for School Improvement through Community Engagement*. Harlow: Pearson Education.

Whitty, G. (2002) *Making Sense of Education Policy*. London: Sage.

Williams, R. (1963) *Culture and Society*. Harmondsworth, Penguin.

Willmott, R. (2002) *Education Policy and Realist Social Theory: Primary Teachers, Child-Centred Philosophy and the New Managerialism*. London: Routledge.

Winnicott, D.W. (1971) *Playing and Reality*. London: Tavistock Publications.

Winstanley, G. (1983[1649]) 'The new law of righteousness', in A. Sharp (ed.), *Political Ideas of the English Civil Wars 1641–1649*. London: Longman.

Witziers, B., Bosker, R. and Kruger, M. (2003) 'Educational leadership and student achievement: the elusive search for an association', *Educational Administration Quarterly*, 39 (3): 398–425.

Woods, G.J. (2003) *Spirituality, Educational Policy and Leadership: A Study of Headteachers*. PhD Thesis, The Open University, Milton Keynes.

Woods, G.J. (2005) 'Going deep: adapting the modernising leadership agenda', *Management in Education*, 18 (4): 28–32.

Woods, P.A. (2000) 'Varieties and themes in producer engagement: structure and agency in the schools public-market', *British Journal of Education*, 21 (2): 219–42.

Woods, P.A. (2001) 'Values-intuitive rational action: the dynamic relationship of instrumental rationality and values insights as a form of social action', *British Journal of Sociology*, 52 (4): 687–706.

Woods, P.A. (2002) 'Space for idealism? Politics and education in the UK', *Edu-*

cational Policy, 16 (1): 118–38.

Woods, P.A. (2003) 'Building on Weber to understand governance: exploring the links between identity, democracy and "inner distance"', *Sociology*, 37 (1): 143–63.

Woods, P.A. (2004) 'Democratic leadership: drawing distinctions with distributed leadership', *International Journal of Leadership in Education: Theory and Practice*, 7 (1): 3–26.

Woods, P.A. (2005) 'Learning and the external environment', in M. Coleman and P. Earley (eds), *Leadership and Management in Education: Cultures, Change and Context*. Oxford: Oxford University Press.

Woods, P.A. and Levačić, R. (2002) 'Raising school performance in the league tables (Part 2): barriers to responsiveness in three disadvantaged schools', *British Educational Research Journal*, 28 (2): 228–47.

Woods, P.A. and Woods, G.J. (2004) 'Modernizing leadership through private participation: a marriage of inconvenience with public ethos?', *Journal of Education Policy*, 19 (6): 643–72.

Woods, P.A., Bennett, N., Wise, C., and Harvey, J.A. (2004) 'Variabilities and dualities in understanding distributed leadership: findings from a systematic literature review', *Educational Management, Administration and Leadership*, 32 (4): 439–57.

Woods, P.A., Castle, F., Cooper, D., Evans, J. and Glatter, R. (2003) 'Pathfinding and diversity: similarities and differences in LEAs' and schools' responses to a government initiative at local level'. Paper presented at British Educational Research Association Conference, Heriot-Watt University, Edinburgh, 11–13 September.

Woods, P.E. (1995) *Creative Teaching in Primary Schools*. Buckingham: Open University Press.

Young, T.L. (1997) 'Leading projects', in M. Preedy, R. Glatter and R. Levačić (eds), *Educational Management Strategy, Quality and Resources*. Buckingham: Open University Press.

Author index

Subject index

Added to the page number 'f' denotes a figure and 't' denotes a table.

academic progress
 and democratic pedagogies xxiii, 63, 71
 see also student achievement
accountabilities of the education profession xix-xx
accountability 74, 94, 102
'active mutual responsibility' 102
activity theory 33
additive leadership 23
adversarial pseudo-participation 83t, 120
affective capacities, duality between rational capacities and 135
agency, complexities and demands of 117–29
aggregation 108
alienation 37
 antithesis of 43
 transcending 37–9, 40–1, 47
analytic concepts and distributed and democratic leadership 34f, 35–9
'anti-structure' 88
apathy 107, 108
 effect on parental participation 79
appropriation of democracy and democratic leadership 75–7
arbitrary power 36, 67, 134
 in the bivalent character of democracy 135
assimilated knowledge 51, 52, 53
associational justice 17, 103

limits 67
'authentic pedagogy' 71
authority 36
 senior figures relinquishing and withdrawing from 108–9
 teacher's 66, 70
 see also externalised authority; 'ideal authority'; internal authority

backing off from power 108–9
 tensions and contradictions 109
benign creativity 25, 119
 basis 38
 encouragement of 117–18
 potential for 3
bivalent structure 87–105
 and arbitrary power 135
 firm framing *see* firm framing
 free space *see* free space
 paradox 133–5
black youth, and school exclusion 100, 103
blurred-status arenas 90–2
 and social interaction and communication 101
bottom-up initiative 107, 121
 duality between lead agency and 136
boundaries of participation 42, 85, 125–7
 opening 118, 129
breaktime for students 89–90
British Idealism 8, 38
broad curriculum 69, 123–4
bureaucracy, persistence of 36, 61

inherent autonomy 42–3
injury, culture of 124–5, 129
'innate ability to be open-minded' 53
inner distance, concept of 38, 43,
  98–9
inner potential, critical reflection on
  112–13
institutional characteristics of
  democratic leadership xviii, 93–7,
  104–5, 133
institutional leadership roles, changes
  in 95
'institutionalised dialogue' 111
instructional leadership 19, 20f
instrumental autonomy 42–3
instrumental rationality 35–6, 37, 40,
  76
  heightened consciousness of 41
  recombination of emotional senses
    and 41
instrumental reasons for democratic
  leadership xxii, 27–31
'the instrumentalisation of the
  expressive' 74
integration of human capacities
  39–42
interests
  competition of 86
  variability 126
internal alignment, rationale xxii
internal authority, distribution 13,
  126
interpersonal concept of leadership
  20
interpersonal pseudo-participation
  83t, 120
intrinsic argument for democratic
  leadership xxii, 32–3
  examination through comparison
    of distributed and democratic
    leadership 33–45
invisible power 61, 81, 126
  control through 67
  of professional control 94
Islam, relationship between
  democracy and 2

knowing-in-action 19
knowledge
  open approach *see* open approach
    to knowledge

perspectives 48–51
knowledge society 31
knowledge-based companies 21
knowledge-based economy 28

labour
  disenchantment 37
  re-enchantment 37, 120
laughter 91
lead agency 121, 128
  duality between bottom-up
    initiative and 136
leaders, rejection of democratic
  leadership 78
leadership xvi–xvii
  in civic republicanism 5t, 7
  in democratic schools 12–13
  emotional aspects 28, 37
  implications of liberal minimalism
    5t, 6
  models *see* models of leadership
  see also additive leadership;
    democratic leadership; dispersed
    leadership; distributed
    leadership; emergent leadership;
    ethically transforming leadership;
    instructional leadership; moral
    leadership; quiet leadership;
    senior leadership; shared
    leadership; teacher leadership;
    transactional leadership;
    transformational leadership
learners
  set of questions for 113
  see also students
learning
  assumptions 28
  links with democratic leadership
    xxiii, 57–72, 136
    democratic pedagogies *see*
      democratic pedagogies
    senior leadership 57–60, 72
    teacher leadership 60–2
  people's inherent potential 127–8
  see also collaborative learning;
    valued learning
learning capacity, transformability 70
legitimacies of power 36
liberal education, paradox 53
liberal minimalism 4–6
  implications for leadership 5t, 6